Question Authority to Think for Yourself

Beverly A. Potter, Ph.D.
Mark J. Estren, Ph.D.

RONIN

Berkeley, California

Question Authority to Think for Yourself

Other Books by Docpotter

Overcoming Job Burnout:
How To Renew Enthusiasm For Work

Finding A Path With A Heart:
How To Go From Burnout To Bliss

The Worrywart's Companion:
21 Ways to Soothe Yourself And Worry Smart

From Conflict To Cooperation:
How To Mediate A Dispute

Get Peak Performance Every Day:
How to Manage Like a Coach

High Performance Goal Setting:
Using Intuition to Conceive & Achieve Your Dreams

Brain Boosters:
Foods & Drugs That Make You Smarter

Drug Testing At Work:
A Guide For Employers And Employees

The Way Of The Ronin:
Riding The Waves Of Change At Work

Turning Around:
Keys To Motivation And Productivity

Preventing Job Burnout:
A Workbook

Youth Extension A-Z

Beyond Consciousness:
What Happens After Death

Patriots Handbook

Spiritual Secrets for Playing the Game of Life

Simple Pleasures

Other Books by Dr. Mark J. Estren

A History of Underground Comics
In a Word

as editor
In Tune with America
Professionally Speaking
Talk Your Way to Success

Question Authority to Think for Yourself

Copyright 2012: Beverly A. Potter

ISBN: 978-1-57951-162-3

Published by

Ronin Publishing, Inc.

PO Box 22900

Oakland, CA 94609

www.roninpub.com

Production:

Cover & Book Design: Beverly A. Potter.
Editor: Mark J. Estren.

Library of Congress Card Number: 2012916229

Distributed to the book trade by PGW/Perseus

Table of Contents

Introduction

Start with the most basic question: why think for yourself? It's troubling, destabilizing and makes personal and professional relationships more difficult. Isn't it better to "go along to get along," to follow the latest trends identified by Google and other tracking services, to watch what others watch, do what others do, accept what others accept, buy what others buy? After all, we want to belong and to be included. Failing to do as others do excludes us, makes us look uninformed or stupid, and puts us at risk of being ignored or marginalized—even being passed over at work for promotions and good assignments.

Whoever or whatever authority may be, it is difficult to question, frequently nonresponsive, and has all sorts of carrots and sticks available to make sure that those who accept it are rewarded and those who question it are punished, through ridicule and ostracism.

Why think for yourself? The answer may seem naïve, New Age-y, overly optimistic, but that does not negate its validity: questioning authority to think for yourself makes you more fully human, more in charge of your own life, more confident, better able to handle the ordinary ups and downs of existence as well as the major changes in trends that seem to occur with

No statement should be believed because it is made by an authority.

-Henry Steele Commager

Foolish faith in author-
ity is the worst enemy
of truth.
—Albert Einstein

increasing frequency. Thinking for yourself makes you better able to make difficult decisions, because your decision-making is rooted in what you think is important, not in what friends or some group has told you to think. Instead of simply accepting whatever may be going on personally, socially or politically, questioning authority to think for yourself enables you to decide whether events are significant or not, whether they matter to you or not, and where you stand, whether you want to participate in them in some way or not—and if so, what form any participation can and should take, and what outcome will be ideal (or at least acceptable) for you and those you care about. It was Benjamin Franklin, now a frequently quoted authority himself, who said, "It is the first responsibility of every citizen to question authority."

Do you sometimes feel like a robot, marching along thoughtlessly in a direction set by others, paying for your group affiliations with a little bit of your spirit? Questioning authority to think for yourself may make you less comfortable with some groups, but you will be more comfortable with yourself—the person with whom you live and interact for 24 hours of every day. Questioning authority to think for yourself means making better decisions for you, rooted in your notions of what is important, in your core values. And this makes it possible to stand up against others when they mindlessly rush over a cliff – and against authority when it acts in malignant ways.

Inspiration for this book comes from Sixties psychologist Timothy Leary's famous slogan: "Think for Yourself; Question Authority." And it is important to note that "question" does not mean "disagree with," but to ask, to uncover and root out so as to understand better—so that you have the foundation upon which to think through your views. Thinking for yourself frequently leads to the same conclusion reached by thoughtlessly following others, because often what others do represents collective wisdom. So questioning authority will frequently lead you to agree with authority, for authority is rooted in common sense and not inherently corrupt and evil, making bad decisions to further invidious goals. Nevertheless, questioning authority to think for yourself is its own reward, even when you simply affirm what others have thought, done or even imposed—because your affirmation is mindful and involved, not slavish or robotic.

For our purposes here, authority refers to anyone advancing a position or argument. It could be a spouse, neighbor, coworker or friend. Authority may also refer to your own ideas, notions, opinions that you hear yourself saying; that you accept, possibly without realizing it, as true, as facts—without questioning. Often

No one should assume that a life of reason is easy. To the contrary, it takes a great deal of courage and honesty. For the only way that you will grow intellectually is by constantly examining your opinions, attacking your prejudices, and completing your journey toward the force of reason. It can be unsettling, and it can be tempting instead to opt for the false comfort of a life without questions. Unfortunately, that's easier to do today than ever. It's possible to live in an echo chamber that serves only to reinforce your high opinion of yourself and what you think. That is a temptation that educated people have a responsibility to reject.

—Condoleezza Rice

Do not believe in anything simply because you have heard it. Do not believe in anything simply because it is spoken and rumored by many. Do not believe in anything simply because it is found written in your religious books. Do not believe in anything merely on the authority of your teachers. Do not believe in traditions because they have been handed down for many generations. But after observation and analysis, when you find that anything agrees with reason and is conducive to the good and benefit of one and all, then accept it and live up to it.

—Timothy Leary

your own ideas, which may have been formed years ago, stand in the way of you thinking for yourself. For example, you may tell yourself that your friends will think you're a hypocrite if you change your mind about something you took a stand on in the past. You may not even be aware that this belief is influencing your current views, keeping you locked into old beliefs, formed long ago.

Come journey with us to explore questioning authority to think for yourself. And keep in mind that what we, your authors, present herein is but one view presented in an authoritative way. So question us, too.

PART ONE

THE POWER OF
AUTHORITY

1

Why We Conform

Do you worry that you are overly influenced by others' opinions and fear you will be rejected or be thought stupid if you reveal the ways that you view things differently? Conformity is essential for society to run smoothly and safely. We obey traffic laws, stand in line to get into a blockbuster movie, or give our seat on the subway to a mother carrying a baby. We feel secure with these rules because we know what to do and that it will be accepted. In a sense we are hard-wired for survival. Conformity enhances survival because it enables us to live in groups. We belong. We're protected from predators. We work together so that the group survives. Others watch our back.

Yet it is understandable to fear being overly conforming, going along too readily, being a "yes man" without personal opinions. Questioning authority to think for yourself does not mean you must come to conclusions different from those of others—but that you come to those conclusions on your own instead of accepting them because friends and family think that way. Thinking for yourself need not ostracize you from friends and coworkers; in fact, if you do come to the same conclusions as others in your social circle, it can cement your friendships more tightly and make you more certain that you really are among like-minded people—true friends, not ones mindlessly marching in the same direction.

We Need to Belong

We all want to belong, to be included. Who wants to be left out and sitting around alone on weekends and holidays? We humans have a deep need to belong. We're tribal animals, after all. Conforming to others' expectations signals to the tribe that "I am like you guys. I am following your rules. I am not a threat. I'm cool." When you conform to expectations of your social circle or work team, others feel more comfortable around you, because they can predict what you will do. So you rise in the pecking order.

Social ostracism was one of the most extreme forms of punishment.

Go against expectations and you risk being excluded, ostracized, even rejected. Social ostracism was one of the most extreme forms of punishment in primitive tribes, described as "being cut dead" by psychologist William James because it was a glimpse into what life would be like if you were nonexistent. There are even reports of wild animals being ostracized by their pack for behaviors that threaten pack survival. Lions, primates, wolves and bees have been reported to use ostracism as a punishment. Ostracized animals lag behind the group and often die from malnutrition or predator attack because they no longer enjoy the protection of their pack. "Ostracism is present in the animal kingdom and is often used to increase a group's chance for survival by basically excluding the weakest link," says Purdue University social psychologist Kipling Williams. "For example, if a lion is hurt and holding the pride up, then that lion may be pushed away."

Groups have norms—values, beliefs, attitudes and behaviors, which may be explicit or implicit. These are the accepted ways of doing things, of dressing, of behavior, of viewpoints. Embracing the social norms leads to approval, while acting against them can result in severe punishments, often exclusion. Norms extend to religious and political beliefs. Norms vary from group to group. Acceptable dress, speech or behavior in one social clique may not be accepted in another. Social norms tend to be unstated, tacitly established and maintained through body language and non-verbal communication.

We learn when and where to say what in the process of interacting with others—what words and topics are acceptable, what to wear, how to sit, what to think. Conforming in these ways brings acceptance and popularity, while ignoring them risks becoming unacceptable, unpopular—even an outcast.

Wanting to be liked and viewed positively seems to be a universal human desire. When we smile at others they tend to like us more. We repeat actions, like smiling, that increase being liked and respected. In this way subtle signs that we are liked, belong and are respected take on tremendous power to influence us. Friends, family and coworkers are inclusive when we act in ways they like—when we conform. The need to belong is so powerful that social isolation, such as being sent to solitary confinement in prison, is considered an especially harsh punishment. Being in isolation weakens our defenses so we are vulnerable to mental and physical illness.

Social behaviors such as smiling are learned without our paying attention to them.We quickly learn "how things are done around here"—we pick it up. We **Are you** fit in, becoming more like those around us, **conforming** in the way we act and think. This is what **without re-** psychologists and sociologists call social **ally deciding** influence. **to do so?**

Thanks to social influence, we do things without thinking, including acceptance of friends' ideas, thoughts, norms and behaviors. Questioning authority to think for yourself requires a willingness to get outside your comfort zone, to realize that you are conforming without really considering the decisions you are making. This does not make conformity bad—it has many benefits. But people who question authority *choose to conform*; they do not simply go along because everyone else goes along.

Conforming Feels Good

When we conform, we find ourselves respected by other conformers, and we look intelligent to them. Interacting Minds Project researchers Chris Frith and Daniel Campbell-Meiklejohn, at Aarhus University in Denmark and University College in London, found that the brain's reward regions lit up strongly when the subject's ratings of pop songs agreed with those of "experts."

"Everyone has an opinion on pop music," says Frith. "And we found that activity in the ventral striatum was very high when the individuals and the experts agreed on their liking of a song." The finding suggests that others' opinions are rewarding when they mirror our own. "Shared opinion is a reward, like food or money," says Campbell-Meiklejohn. "And being a reward, it has the power to influence behavior."

"Social influence affects our behavior. Most of the time, we underestimate the influence of conformity," says Vasily Klucharev, economic psychology researcher at Basel University in Switzerland, who studies the brain mechanisms of social influence and how they can alter our behavior. Conformity is an automatic process that happens whether we're aware of it or not, which may explain why we don't realize it when our behavior is influenced by what our peers do. "It is a rapid learning—a basic and quick process. And it's one that can have quite an impact on our behaviors," he says.

Our social "smarts" are derived experientially. Through trial and error we come to know what types of people we can and cannot discuss certain topics with, when and where we can wear certain attire, and so forth.

Downside of Conformity

But conformity has a downside. We feel trapped. We feel like a robot, a bee in a hive, not like an individual. Groups can do bad things, such as what happened in William Golding's novel, *Lord of the Flies*, about a group of boarding-school boys, stranded on a remote island and removed from the larger world and its controls, that tries to govern itself—with disastrous results. New norms quickly evolved, with the boys looking down upon

weakness, leading them to hunt down a weak boy, threatening to ritually kill him.

We feel like a robot, a bee in a hive, not like an individual.

Whether in political or social circumstances, pressure to conform is strong, and difficult to overcome. Fears of exclusion and loss of respect run deep. Being true to yourself, knowing that you are acting in accordance with your values, helps to inoculate you against being marginalized. But no one says that it is easy to be an independent thinker. In fact, being seen as a rebel could get you locked up as "crazy."

2
You Must Be Crazy

As if the risk of being ostracized weren't bad enough, going against the social grain can get you labeled as "crazy." Folks who voice the "wrong" views, ask the "wrong" questions, are marginalized, shunned and may even be deemed mentally ill. People who challenge the consensus view, the way others see things, are often considered to be nuts, kooks, crazies, loons. According to the psychotherapist's bible, *Diagnostic and Statistical Manual of Mental Disorders* (DSM-IV), people who question authority are "dysfunctional"—afflicted with "oppositional defiant disorder" (ODD)—and "exhibit a pattern of negativistic, defiant, disobedient and hostile behavior toward authority figures." Symptoms include expressing anger, deliberately annoying people, blaming others for all that goes wrong, and being unable to take "no" for an answer. People with ODD are contrary, stubborn, and throw temper tantrums.

Being an independent thinker sounds romantic. Wow, cool, man! But, as Leary observed, independent thinkers often endure long periods of quiescence, obscurity, even a kind of social disgrace. As virtual outcasts, feeling agonizingly out of step, independent thinkers are shunned, ostracized, often without anyone explicitly saying what is going on or giving any reason.

Authorities have even lobotomized "rebels"

> *There's an ominous tendency to call "insane" those we don't agree with.*
>
> —Timothy Leary

What are you hoping to achieve by reading a book about questioning authority? who refused to embrace consensus reality. There is a long and sordid history of governments using psychiatry for political repression. In one fictional but dramatic example, Murphy, who ran afoul of Nurse Ratched in Ken Kesey's *One Flew Over the Cuckoo's Nest*, is a case in point. In the Soviet Union, thousands of political prisoners were detained in mental hospitals, isolated from friends and family, and in many cases forcibly medicated. Nazi Germany murdered nearly two hundred thousand psychiatric patients. Governments are well known to repress people who have a pattern of negativistic, defiant, disobedient and hostile behavior toward authority figures.

Outcasts

Be honest with yourself. What are you hoping to achieve by reading a book about questioning authority? You may find it easier to set this book aside and join the ranks of the well-adjusted, acceptable group-thinkers. This may be even more important if you are female, since women are still generally expected to be more compliant than men.

Philosophers who encourage people to question authority to think for themselves are considered to be dangerous, heretical, immoral, even insane. One such dangerous character was Socrates, who was accused of corrupting impressionable youths by encouraging them to question authority—his own authority included—to think for themselves, and refusing to cease this blasphemous behavior.

President Richard Nixon called Timothy Leary "the most dangerous man alive" because he constantly encouraged youth to question authority. Leary taught that what we accept as objective reality is only a construction of our minds. The only way to realize our true selves is to question everything we have learned from parents, teachers, politicians. Socrates' approach, the Socratic Method—"knowledge of not-knowing"—questions unquestioned "truths" and keeps questioning until students discover for themselves that they actually "know nothing" in the sense of absolute knowledge. Leary's approach provoked people to question their models of reality imposed by authorities, encouraging them "to create their own funnier, sexier, more optimistic realities."

When Nixon called me that, I was thrilled. The President of the United States, whom many Americans and the rest of the world thought was a crazed, psychotic dan- ger, for him to be calling me that, I, that's my Nobel Prize, that's my bumper sticker, that's my trophy on the wall.

—Timothy Leary

In PBS's obituary of Leary by Charlayne Hunter-Gault, psychiatrist Robert Coles said "This is not frivolous behavior. This is dangerous behavior. This is destructive behavior, and I think the most interesting question of all is: Why have we paid so much attention to him and people like him in the Sixties and to this day?"

3

What's Wrong With Being Wrong?

Do you hold back from questioning others for fear of making a mistake and seeming foolish, even considered ridiculous by friends and colleagues? Wouldn't it be easier to shut up and fit in, so you will be respected by others, be called on more often in meetings, be considered a team player? These considerations should not be minimized—humans are social animals. There are risks is going against the herd. It is much easier just to "go along to get along."

Many elements of accepted wisdom are in fact correct; this explains why questioning authority to think for yourself often leads to the same conclusion that others agree on simply on the basis that authority says it, or because it has always been that way (tradition), or because there has been a proclamation in a book or other respected source (Bible, Koran, textbooks, *The New York Times*). Independent thinkers may fear being wrong and are sometimes wrong, but they pursue their own analysis anyway, sometime becoming defiant. For example, President Andrew Jackson, tired of having his intelligence dismissed through his often being mocked as a notoriously poor speller, once commented, "It's a damn poor mind that can only think of one way to spell a word."

Much of accepted wisdom is correct.

Mistakes Valuable

Thinking independently requires making mistakes. Errors are the bridge to new understanding. "The man who makes no mistakes does not usually make anything," said American lawyer and diplomat Edward John Phelps in the late nineteenth century, and the reason for this is clear: questioning authority to think for yourself inevitably leads down some blind alleys as you ferret out your understanding of the matter. Thomas Edison is famous for saying, while working methodically to find a usable filament for the light bulb, "I have not failed. I've just found 10,000 ways that won't work." But a comment from him that is equally relevant is, "It is astonishing what an effort it seems to be for many people to put their brains definitely and systematically to work."

To swear off making mistakes is very easy. All you have to do is swear off having ideas.

—Leo Burnett

What makes questioning authority so hard? The difficulties start in childhood, when parents—the first and most powerful authority figures—show children "the way things are." This is a necessary element of learning language and socialization, and certainly most things learned in early childhood are noncontroversial: the English alphabet starts with A and ends with Z, the numbers 1 through 10 come before the numbers 11 through 20, and so on. Children, however, will spontaneously question things that are quite obvious to adults and even to older kids. The word "why?" becomes a challenge, as in, "Why is the sky blue?" Answers such as "because it just is" or "because I say so" tell children that they must unquestioningly accept what authorities say "just because," and children who persist in their questioning are likely to find themselves dismissed or yelled at for "bothering" adults with "meaningless"

Freedom is not worth having if it does not include the freedom to make mistakes.

—Mahatma Gandhi

or "unimportant" questions. But these questions are in fact perfectly reasonable. Why is the sky blue? Many adults do not themselves know the answer. And who says the sky's color needs to be called "blue," anyway? How do we know that what one person calls "blue" is the same color that another calls "blue"? The scientific answers come from physics, but those are not the answers that children are seeking. They are trying to understand the world, and no matter how irritating the repeated questions may become to stressed and time-pressed parents, it is important to take them seriously to encourage kids to question authority to think for themselves.

Thinking for yourself to question authority as an adult requires recapturing some of the sense of curiosity, even of wonder, that is wrung out of kids as they grow older and go through systematic education—which includes subtle indoctrination, not necessarily intentional, in "the way things are" and "the way they should be" (which are not the same thing, but are often presented as if they are identical). Kids do not fear guessing wrong, at least until they begin taking standardized tests, and adults who think for themselves to question authority need to learn, or re-learn, the fearlessness of inquiries that may lead nowhere, or to the wrong conclusions.

Errors are inevitable when children question parental authority to think for themselves. So what? "Unless we teach our children how to embrace mistakes and defeats, our self-confident little dynamo may learn to fear ridicule and reprimand," says Elisa Medhus, M.D., a family-practice physician from Houston and author of *The Importance of Making Mistakes: Helping Kids Learn from Failure*. Medhus goes on with the cautionary remark, "Eventually, he may even rely on outside evaluation to assess his own performance, measure his self-worth, and shape his future choices." And this is exactly what happens with far too many adults.

> *We learn from failure, not from success.*
>
> —Bram Stoker author of *Dracula*

So what, exactly, is the problem with being wrong? Well, nothing. We need errors to correct so that we can learn. Unfortunately, far too many of us develop a notion that we must perform perfectly at all times. When we don't, when we fail to meet our unrealistic expectations of ourselves, we too often feel humiliated. It is this tendency to feel humiliated when viewed as less than perfect that sets us up to be especially susceptible to the power of ridicule.

Question Yourself

Notice mistakes you make in everyday life—situations that don't go well and things you said and did that turned out to be "wrong." Question what happened, paying close attention to how you viewed the situation or issue—that is, question your own authority. What did you tell yourself about the situation or issue? How did you know this to be true? What other ways might you have described the situation to yourself? How did what you told yourself influence your actions, those of others, the outcome?

Do not beat yourself up if, in retrospect, you find that what you told yourself about the situation or issue was wrong: getting upset at yourself accomplishes nothing and actually prevents you from learning from the mistake. And that is the important thing: to learn from the mistake. Remember the phrase: trial and error? This means to do something and then correct it, improve it, refine it. This is how we learn and progress. It is this learning that gives mistakes their value. Without the mistake, you have nothing to improve upon.

Alice's Story

After years as an instructor, Alice was promoted to department head at a state university. As part of her supervisory responsibilities, Alice closely examined the curriculum developed by the instructors and periodically observed their classes to be sure students were getting the best possible education. She gave teachers well-thought-out and careful performance reviews that were sensitive to the nuances of their courses. Alice was surprised and dismayed when instructors found new positions and student feedback forms had comments about class that were often negative.

Consider Alice as a college administrator—an authority. Questioning herself, Alice realized that she assumed she could teach the courses better than the instructors could. While she may, in fact, have been a more skilled instructor, she realized that she had been communicating superiority—and the judgment accompanying it—which was not helpful and was, in fact, a failure on her part. Her visits to classes, intended to be unobtrusive, affected the teachers and the dynamics of the classrooms negatively because of the possibility that she might judge the teachers harshly, a worry that the students sensed in the instructors.While Alice's performance reviews were intelligent, careful and sensitive, not harsh, that did not overcome the environment she created in her audits of the classes.

Alice learned from examining the mistaken assumptions behind her auditing of instructors' classes. She still believed that she could teach courses better than her instructors, but she realized that she needed to encourage different teaching styles. She also realized that, even if instructors did not do as well as she herself would, they needed to make their own mistakes to learn and improve. When Alice changed her supervisory approach to give the teachers more flexibility, turnover in her department decreased, and student satisfaction improved.

Alice's story contains an important lesson in thinking for yourself to question authority—a lesson that should be taught in childhood and remembered by adults. Perhaps the most important "error inoculation" you can give children is not to rescue them from every problem, challenge or conflict. Stepping in as a *deus ex machina*—a "god from the machine" that appears from on high to solve the problems of mere mortals—tells kids that the "right" result matters more than the process of working out a solution. This is a lesson easily carried into adult life—it leads people to look to leaders, including self-proclaimed ones, for solutions to difficult problems.

But the process of working out a solution yourself is a highly valuable one. Yes, it can be messy, since it includes errors and miscalculations. But it ultimately leads to answers thought up by the children or adults themselves, such as the teachers working in Alice's department. Those answers may appear only after considerable difficulty and frustration. But giving people of any age the benefit of making mistakes helps encourage them to think for themselves, accept the inevitability of error, and be unafraid to question authority.

As Alice discovered, stepping back and letting others make their own mistakes is not easy. It may be true in the grand scheme of one's life that "the only things one never regrets are one's mistakes," as Oscar Wilde said, but when we make mistakes, or watch as others make them when we could help those others avoid them, they do feel regrettable. Making mistakes when questioning authority as adults feels worse: those in power will go out of their way to make those who question or challenge them feel simply awful, and there are powerful social conformity pressures among friends, colleagues, members of any peer group. But here is something that can help both kids and adults: Norton Juster's classic book, *The Phantom Tollbooth*. Although theoretically written for children, it is packed

> *Anyone who has never made a mistake has never tried anything new.*
>
> —Albert Einstein

with advanced ideas about questioning authority and thinking for yourself—and written so kids can read it, parents can read it with them, and adults can read it on their own, with people of every age benefiting from its wisdom. The book is cast as a fable about the rescue of princesses named Rhyme and Reason from a land that has lost sight of both, making the story an allegory that is just as valuable for adults as for children. Pay special attention to this passage:

> *"It has been a long trip," said Milo, climbing onto the couch where the princesses sat; "but we would have been here much sooner if I hadn't made so many mistakes. I'm afraid it's all my fault.*
>
> *You must never feel badly about making mistakes," explained Reason quietly, "as long as you take the trouble to learn from them. For you often learn more by being wrong for the right reasons than you do by being right for the wrong reasons."*

Psychiatrist Carl Jung made a similar point in a less literary and strictly adult way that ties directly into Edison's many thousands of filament attempts: "Mistakes are, after all, the foundations of truth, and if a man does not know what a thing is, it is at least an increase in knowledge if he knows what it is not."

4
Obedience to Authority

Do you struggle with pressure from friends, from co-workers, from family, from supervisors to conform and accept their way of thinking and doing things? Do you feel pressure to stop questioning and to accept what others tell you is so? Do you catch yourself going along to fit in? Confronting pressures to conform is a constant struggle. If you are like most people, you'll sometimes conform and later wish you'd thought to question. Stop beating yourself up! Questioning authority to think for yourself is not all or nothing; it is a skill, which we get better at with practice—a lot of practice.

If you're like most people, you don't want to be excluded or treated with contempt because you question others. You may be tempted, again and again, to stop questioning the "way we do things" and simply go along to get along. Yet, when you do so you feel like a "sheeple" with no individual thoughts or ideas, just bleating back what others say. Keep in mind that when you question PC-isms and other accepted ways of thinking about things, you often come to the same conclusions that others unquestioningly

The formula for failure is trying to please everybody with everything that you do. So the formula for success must be the opposite of that, which is not being consumed with what other people are thinking, and listening to your own inner voice.

—Dr. Wayne Dyer

accept—but they are your conclusions, not ones imposed on you by someone in authority.

What is Authority?

Authority is the right and ability to control, command, or determine the acceptable responses of others. Authority involves a *right or legitimate claim* to lead or rule in some sphere. For example, judges have the authority to sentence you to a prison term, but not the right to determine what car you must drive. Authority includes the *ability or power* to exercise that claim.

Consider Galileo. With the use of his telescope, which he invented, Galileo proved Copernicus' theory that the Earth revolves around the Sun. Because this went against the Roman Catholic Church's view, Galileo was put on trial for heresy for challenging the Church's authority. He was convicted and condemned, and his writings were burned. Of course, Galileo was right and the Church authorities were wrong! Nevertheless, Galileo spent his remaining years under house arrest—which shows what can happen when you challenge authority. It took the church more than 300 years to acknowledge that Galileo was correct—because church leaders feared that admitting the church's mistake would undermine their authority.

Authority is not a quality one person 'has,' in the sense that he has property or physical qualities. Authority refers to an interpersonal relation in which one person looks upon another as somebody superior to him.

—Erich Fromm

Authority also refers to recognized expertise in a topic. For example, a professor who studied primate-mating behavior for 30 years would be considered an "authority" on the subject, and trusted to give correct information. Of course, authorities can be wrong. Academic librarians rely heavily on the concept of authority when evaluating information. Authority for librarians is understood to be a reviewed and reputable source. Scholars trust sources that have such authority over those that lack it. Whatever authority is, we like it.

Obeying Authority

Government is made up of people—individuals. Sometimes people in government do harmful things. Authorities can be power-hungry, as with totalitarian governments. If you're like most people, you're sure that you would resist if government—bureaucrats with authority—pressed you to do something harmful to another person. But maybe you shouldn't be so sure. Yale psychologist Stanley Milgram's research revealed that all people—even the most decent individuals—have the potential to act in harmful ways when told to do so by an authority. In Milgram's classic study, 62% of college-student subjects were willing to administer a fatal shock when told to do so by an authority. Milgram's experiment has been repeated with the same results with subjects drawn from all walks of life.

> *The ultimate authority must always rest with the individual's own reason and critical analysis.*
>
> —Dalai Lama

Subjects were told the experiment was an investigation of memory and involved punishment of mistakes; then they were introduced to a confederate working with Milgram who they were told was another "subject." The confederate was supposedly picked as the "Learner," through a rigged lottery, while the real subject was "selected" as the Teacher.

Next, the Teacher (subject) watched as the Learner (confederate) was strapped into a constraining electric-shock device in the next room that featured a large dial indicating 15 to 450 volts. To reinforce the belief that the shock generator was real, Teachers—the actual subjects—were given a mildly painful 45-volt shock.

The task was for the Teacher to quiz the Learner on a list of word-pairs Learners had been told to memorize. When the Learner gave the wrong answer, a Professor—the authority, wearing a white lab coat—instructed the Teacher to increase the voltage level of the shock.

Milgram's interest was in studying whether Teachers (the actual subjects) would challenge the authority to stop the test, or would comply with the authority and inflict extremely painful shocks on the Learner, who could be heard begging and screaming from the other room to be let out (this agonized pleading was actually a tape recording of the Learner's voice).

When a Teacher protested, "I can't go on!" the Professor replied in a calm, firm voice, "Yes, there is some pain, but the experiment requires that you continue. Please go on." Should a Teacher protest, "I'm sorry, I am not going to continue. I don't want to cause this pain. I can't do this," the Professor replied firmly, "Just go on."

At 225 volts Teachers heard a taped recording of the Learner crying, "Let me out. I won't take this." After several voltage level increases, the Learner begged to be released. After banging on the wall and complaining about a heart problem, the Learner was silent—leaving the Teacher to wonder if the Learner was unconscious, or even dead.

Some subjects began questioning the experiment at 135 volts, but most continued when assured by the Professor that they would not be held responsible. A few subjects laughed nervously and exhibited other signs of stress. Shockingly, 65 percent (26 of 40) of subjects administered the massive 450-volt shock—even while declaring themselves uncomfortable doing so.

Ordinary people, simply doing their jobs, and without any particular hostility on their part, can become agents in a terrible destructive process. Moreover, even when the destructive effects of their work become patently clear, and they are asked to carry out actions incompatible with fundamental standards of morality, relatively few people have the resources needed to resist authority

—Stanley Milgram

Coming only 15 years after Hitler's Holocaust, Milgram's findings horrified the world: when told to do so by an authority, the majority of people violate their deepest moral values and inflict severe pain, even death, on others.

You may think you would never have gone along with authority in this experiment, but be honest and question yourself. Have you ever sat silently while your boss berated one of your colleagues for some minor issue? Did you ever remain silent while the teacher at school took another student to task over expressing an unpopular political view? Somehow in these situations we can find ourselves paralyzed. They are authorities; we've been trained our whole lives to do what they say, to obey, not to question. Understanding that almost everyone has faced this dilemma is a step toward developing awareness of the entire issue: the potential of being railroaded by authority simply because it is authority.

It can be a matter of self-preservation not to talk against the boss or the teacher; no one will quarrel with that decision. Questioning is one thing; what you do with the answers is another. Questioning does not necessarily have to be an out-loud challenge. It is an attitude. Rather than conforming, obeying in a kneejerk way as we have been trained, questioning is an awareness of what is going on and wondering about it. You may choose to remain silent, even when the boss or teacher is being unfair, for example. It is better to choose consciously, for any number of personal reasons, including self-preservation, than to obey mindlessly. Perhaps you will speak privately to the boss, or console your colleague—or prepare your resume.

Questioning Is Natural

We emerged at birth into a world of chaos, awakening to consciousness to find ourselves residing in something like a biochemical robot, without benefit of any operating manual. What's going on here? Who am I? Where am I going? We had to discover who and what we are at the same time that we faced the challenge of learning how to operate our bio-robot, while also figuring out how to play the game of life.

Throughout history as our species has faced the frightening terrorizing fact that we do not know who we are or where we are going in this ocean of chaos, it has been the authorities—political, religious, educational authorities—who attempted to comfort us by giving us order, rules, regulations, informing—forming our minds into their view of reality.

—Timothy Leary

Frightened and overwhelmed, we look to authority for security and comfort. Authorities tell us the rules of the game and provide laws, regulations, myths, and customs for playing it. We believe authority and trust that what it says is true. We rely upon authority to tell us the score—beginning with Mom and Dad.

As humans, we have an ability to self-program and a desire to self-define, which "kicks in" when we're about two years old—sometimes called "the terrible twos." Curiosity is hard-wired. Children constantly ask, "Why?" We naturally explore and inquire about the mysterious ocean of chaos in which we've awakened. This natural inclination to question and explore puts us at cross-purposes with society— the authorities. Authority fears inquiry because it inevitably challenges the established order of things. Authority wants stability. Questions hold the catalyst for change, threatening authority. Remember what happened to Socrates.

Inquiry can lead to change. What if I question this long-held assumption, this way of life that I've always believed to be right and true? Friends and family might reject me. I could be censured by colleagues and condemned, even hounded, by authorities. PC-think—accepting the prevailing views of others—is much safer. Why rock the boat and risk falling or being thrown overboard when it's easier to go along to get along?

Why Question Authority?

Question authority not because it is authority but because it is through questioning that you think for yourself—the questioning stimulates thinking. Sometimes authority may be wrong, as with Galileo, or have tainted, even evil, motives; then thinking for yourself to question authority is vital. But how can you do so when authority is malignant, if you don't question it when it is benign? Furthermore, what's the alternative? To accept what authority says without question, telling yourself that authority operates from benevolent motives, at least most of the time? That's being a "sheeple," not a thinking person.

Without questioning, we have the potential to slip into obedience that can lead to hurting others. If we do not make it a habit to question authority regularly to think for ourselves, how do we know when to trust and when to question? As Milgram demonstrated, when an authority figure says it's okay to hurt others, most people will do it. Not all the subjects in Milgram's experiments obeyed the Professor when they heard someone crying in pain, but the disobedient ones were in the minority. One theory is that reliance on authority relieves us from responsibility for our actions. Another theory is that we are trained to accept authority. Supervisors chill your job prospects if they write in an evaluation "has problems with authority." Even today, in our society, girls, more than boys, are subtly taught to accept things passively, not to question—that is considered "aggressive," and aggression is not feminine; obedience is.

> *Question with boldness. Don't just accept what those professors say. Question. Read what they say not to read. Oh, yeah, and read what they tell you to read. Then ask why? Question with boldness.*
>
> —Glenn Beck

Simply questioning authority can be very anxiety-provoking after years of being trained to accept it passively. This goes back to childhood: remember what happened when you "talked back" to your parents? What do you do now when your kid talks back?

Then there are the rebels. Rebels rebel—with or without a cause. Always rebelling is not independence; it's rebelliousness—always being contrary, regardless of the situation. That's mindless reactivity. The mind is not engaged; just the kneejerk. Independence is questioning— mulling over. Weighing. Contemplating. Thinking. Flushing out your own stand on the issue. Sometimes your views will be in line with  others'; other times they will be divergent. This sort of mindful questioning is the sign of an independent thinker—of thinking for yourself. The tool of thinking is asking questions, not making statements. Asking questions opens up the mind; making statements closes it. Socrates told us this.

Whom to Question

An authority may be a spouse, neighbor, coworker or friend advancing a position or argument. It may be a parent or a supervisor, or another person whose authority comes from a position of power over you. Or it may be an official societal authority, such as a police officer, IRS agent, bank loan officer or someone similar. Authority may also refer to your own ideas and notions, opinions that you hear yourself saying; that you accept, possibly without realizing it, as true, as facts—without questioning.

You may have formed certain beliefs and ideas years ago that stand in the way of what you want to accomplish today. For example, you may tell yourself that you should never take out a loan on a car because it is too expensive. Buying a used car with all cash is the only way to go. This may have been a good guideline

Questioning your own opinions and how you formed them is probably your most important challenge.

when you were a college student: if the old car broke down you could leave it and ride a bike to class until you got the bucks together to get it repaired. Years later when you are ferrying kids around in an unreliable old car this may no longer be a good guiding rule. Such old beliefs need questioning and updating. Maybe with kids in a car, it is more important to have a reliable car, even if it means having a car loan with monthly payments.

Question yourself first, last, and again. Examine your ideas, values, and beliefs. Samuel Johnson said, "The unexamined life is not worth living." The purpose is not to create self-doubt, but the opposite—confidence in your opinions. The more you question, the better you understand how you've come to a belief and why you feel confident in it—even if others believe differently. You will probably find that some of your beliefs don't add up, even if they once did. If so, modify or discard them.

What to Question

Questioning your own opinions and how you formed them is probably your most important challenge. It is amazing how ideas can infiltrate our minds without our realizing it. Major offenders are the media, which are everywhere. We are bombarded with viewpoints coming at us from our huge array of electronic gadgets, as well as from TV and radio. Every message has a viewpoint behind it; for example, advertisements have hidden assumptions, like "sexy is good," which is used constantly by marketers. We spent about two decades with parents who were indoctrinating us in how to live and what to think.

The influence of peers, as we all know, is huge. There is no end of the need to question our own authority—the things we believe and accept as true, which we may have absorbed unwittingly.

Develop a habit of questioning—not challenging, but mindful questioning. These are clues that point to fuzzy thinking: beliefs, biases, assumptions, inferences, and fallacies. To get beyond fuzzy thinking, be alert to generalities and exaggerations. Statements that begin with a generality like "Everyone knows..." are hollow. Ask for specifics. It can also be helpful to imagine the other person's perspective, which can help uncover the motive or reasoning behind authorities' stance. If the situation becomes heated, pull back by relaxing and breathing slowly and deeply. Stay in control of yourself and you will be better equipped to handle whatever is going on.

Gather facts before judging—it is hard to make a sound judgment without adequate information. It is helpful to assume there is no one "right" view. Recognize that authorities speak from their own experience, which may be right for them, even if not for you.

5

Are Your Beliefs Yours?

How do you know if your beliefs are yours or if you picked them up from parents, teachers, friends, coworkers and other "authorities"? When you are surrounded by people who hold the same beliefs as you do, those views are constantly reinforced until they do, indeed, feel true—real. There is simply no contrast, nothing to remind you to question. Independent thinkers work at independent thinking, reminding themselves to question established beliefs, especially their own.

You have your way. I have my way. As for the right way, the correct way, the only way: it does not exist.

—Friedrich Nietzsche

Independent thinking is not spontaneous behavior, but learned and continuously improved—through practice— like any other skill. A good place to practice is uprooting and questioning your own hidden beliefs that serve as an invisible authority directing you.

What Are Beliefs?

Beliefs are assumed truths. Everything we think we know is a belief. Beliefs are a kind of bedrock to which we anchor our understanding of experiences and knowledge. Our beliefs are what we assume to be true; other people's beliefs are what they assume to be true. Brain scientist John C. Lilly, M.D, says, "In the province of the mind, what is believed to be true is true or becomes true." In other words, believing has a way of making us see what we believe as real, as true.

Believing Is Seeing

Beliefs are a kind of perceptual filter through which information received from the outside world is processed—and colored by the belief in the process. Beliefs have the power to guide us, but also the potential to imprison us. Once we believe something, we tend to keep on believing it, even in the face of contrary evidence. We filter out and ignore—even distort—information that does not confirm our beliefs—imprisoning us as our minds shut out data that challenge our beliefs. Worse, beliefs become woven into a wider web of beliefs—a belief system, an ideology—so that it is difficult to question one belief without shaking everything up.

When is the last time you thought about your beliefs? Beliefs feel true, but "feeling right" doesn't make them so. We see what we expect to see—what we believe is true. Actually, beliefs are a collection of agreed-upon ideas—what Lilly calls a "consensus reality." The consensus behind commonly held beliefs elevates them to a kind of self-imposed authority. Our own beliefs are an authority we should frequently question and come back to question again and again, because we change and evolve. Unquestioned beliefs can hold us back and lock us in.

Bias

Bias is an unstated belief in a particular view. Bias colors claims and conclusions by putting subtle emphasis on certain ideas while ignoring others. Bias is one-sided, tending toward partiality, preference, and prejudice.

I've changed my mind a few times. One thing I can say for sure is that I've never changed it while surrounded by people who agree with me.

—Timothy Leary

44

> *Do not fear to be eccentric in opinion, for every opinion now accepted was once eccentric.*
>
> —Bertrand Russell

It is important to realize, however, that the fact that a person is biased doesn't mean that the person's argument is wrong. Bias has no bearing on validity of the argument in question. Bias itself does not invalidate the logic of an argument or the validity of the supporting evidence. Dismissing an argument *prima facie* without considering its merits simply because the argument or its presenter appears biased is to make a common logical fallacy. The rational way to determine the validity and accuracy of any assertion is to notice the bias and examine the relevant evidence.

Actually, a strongly biased person is usually pretty knowledgeable and can be helpful in exploring the truth about something. For example, a longtime baseball enthusiast is more likely to have solid information on the benefits to kids of playing sports than someone with no interest in sports at all. By comparison, people who are only slightly biased are more likely to rely on fanciful and invalid reasoning to support their opinions than those who are strongly biased, who are usually more informed.

Questions to Uncover Bias

When you listen to someone's presentation, or prepare one yourself, look for underlying beliefs that are important to making the argument but are not actually stated. Notice ways you may be fighting what the other person is saying. There is a collision of biases whenever people express themselves to others: the biases of the one doing the speaking or writing and those of the one doing the listening or reading. What is important to understand is that noticing biases—yours included—does not diminish the other person's view, but helps you to listen better as well as to ask better questions.

To uncover those filters, ponder questions such as: What facts have been omitted? What additional information is needed to be more complete? What words shaped my (positive or negative) impression of the person's comments? Use these questions to ferret out your own biases.

Assumptions

An assumption is a thought that lies behind a belief—it is something taken for granted or presupposed in forming that belief. We assume that our beliefs are true and use assumptions to interpret the world about us. Beliefs, and their underlying assumptions, can be justified or unjustified, depending upon whether we do or do not have good reasons for them.

The assumptions underlying beliefs influence the way you and other people express their ideas. Identifying the beliefs helps you get at the assumptions. For example, if someone says, "I work my butt off and then must pay taxes to support people who sit on their butts and don't work," the underlying belief may be that people who work hard should not have to support people who don't work. What is the assumption beneath that belief? The speaker may assume that people who don't work are lazy and don't want to work. Understanding the belief and the foundational assumption beneath it helps you decide whether you agree with the statement or not.

Men become civilized, not in proportion to their willingness to believe, but in their readiness to doubt.

—H.L. Mencken

An assumption is an unstated premise in an argument, something the speaker has left unsaid. It is the missing step in the argument, a missing reason needed for the argument to support the conclusion.

Take the statement, "Taxes are too high." That is a forthright statement of belief. But what is the underlying assumption? There could be several: that money collected from taxes is used for unimportant things; that taxes take away from what's important, such as hiring people; that tax money is wasted; that the tax-collection system itself is unfair; and so on. Questioning the underlying assumption supporting the belief, not simply reacting to the statement with "no, they're not" or "yes, they are" helps you to think through what you think about paying taxes. Even if you agree that taxes are too high, your underlying assumptions may be different from those of the speaker. You may think they are wasted on a bloated government bureaucracy, while the speaker may run a small business and be reluctant to hire more people because of the tax burden. Rooting out assumptions helps you figure out "where the person is coming from" to get to the core issues in an argument.

We all make assumptions. Assumptions and inferences permeate our lives precisely because we cannot act without them. We make judgments, form interpretations, and come to conclusions based on our beliefs. For example, if you hold a pencil and let go of it, you assume that it will fall. Theoretically, this need not happen: if all the molecules in the pencil happened to move in an upward direction simultaneously, the pencil might hover. But this is so unlikely that there is no need to think about it –except as a mind-expanding exercise. It is always useful to identify our beliefs and assumptions and question them, if only to reaffirm their validity.

Our assumptions are not always justifiable. There may be little actual evidence in support. Ferreting out our assumptions can be surprisingly difficult, because they are rooted in a belief system formed over years that we take to be true because we don't examine or question deep-seated beliefs – since we are largely unaware of them. It is a little like the way that we don't notice the air around us, except in a strong wind or when there is a smell.

> *Assumptions are like the strong undercurrents of a gentle river. On the surface the river appears to be flowing with placid, warm water. Underneath the calm, the current is colder water pushing with power and force. Our assumptions lie underneath the surface of our thinking and actions. If we are unaware of the deep currents of our assumptions, we go forward with a limited capacity to respond to the bend in the river.*
>
> —Donna Zajonc
> *Leadership Matters*

The Because Test

When listening to people speaking about their views on something, listen for the reasons given for the opinion or statement and then listen for the conclusion. Make a habit of asking, "What's missing?" "What's not being reported?" The "Because Test" can help reveal unstated assumptions. Insert the word "because" into the passage directly before the phrase that you think is a "reason." Then identify the unspoken assumption needed to get from the reason to the conclusion. "Rich people should pay more taxes because..." Because what? Because they do not pay enough now? Because they have it easier than other people? Because the Gospel of Luke says, "From everyone who has been given much, much will be required"? Because it is unfair to have much when others have little?

Search and Question

The problem with assumptions is that they are influential foundations of belief and are hidden, unstated, and taken for granted—unnoticed and unquestioned. When we have made a judgment about others, we tend to look for things about people to support our judgments of them. Our view is not objective, because everything that people do is tainted with the labels—good or bad—that we have stamped on them

Develop a habit of questioning ideas you believe to be true. Ask yourself, "Do I know this as a fact? Or am I making an assumption? If this is a fact, according to what source?" You will be surprised at how often you discover assumptions you hadn't realized you were relying upon. "Only rich people can afford to have money in the stock market, so profits from stocks should be taxed at higher rates to make rich people pay more." Think for yourself, investigate, and you will find that 54% of Americans had money in stocks as of mid-2011. How does that information affect your opinion?

Over-Flowing Cup

The Seeker and Shaman Woman were enjoying a cup of tea in the garden. As the Shaman Woman poured tea into the Seeker's cup, he asked, "What is wisdom? What is enlightenment? Should I know everything? Help me understand, Shaman Woman." Saying nothing, the Shaman Woman continued pouring the tea into the cup, which filled, then overflowed. "What are you doing? The cup is overflowing!" he exclaimed. "Like this cup," the Shaman Woman replied, "you are full of your assumptions and preconceptions. You must empty your mind before you can learn.

There is nothing wrong with making assumptions. The problem comes when you think and act as if the assumption is a fact. Unfortunately, many of our beliefs are based on unconscious, hidden assumptions. We can't question assumptions when we don't recognize they exist.Hidden assumptions can be very difficult to recognize and correct. What you assume may be only a guess or a probability, or it may be something that you have accepted because "everybody agrees." Identify what "everybody agrees upon" as an assumption, and ask yourself what the consequences will be if the assumption is incorrect. Then decide if the assumption is one you want to hold onto – it may be a long-cherished one that no longer fits today's circumstances.

Question Often

Things that were true for you many years ago may no longer have the same power. Develop a habit of regularly questioning your assumptions so that you can find values and beliefs you hold without realizing it. You may be relying upon assumptions you've accepted unquestioningly from authorities, like your parents, for example. Examine the assumptions behind the choices and decisions you make, and the goals and aspirations you hold. For example, you may avoid living in cities because you "know" they are dirty and crime-ridden. That may have been your parents' belief based on their experiences—and it may even have been accurate at the time. But is it still accurate in all cities? You may have been making lifestyle decisions for decades based on assumptions that were never valid, or that are or were valid for someone else, or that made sense in the past but no longer do.

Question Assumptions

Just because you question an assumption doesn't mean you should throw it out the window. You may reaffirm an assumption with some updating, or you may reframe the assumption, or you may throw it out. Such adjustments are called growing, evolving. We make assumptions about other people's intentions, which are often wrong. When you approach people with a negative view of their intentions, they sense it and tend to go on the defensive, often called getting off on the wrong foot.

By contrast, when you question your assumptions about another's intention, it is easier to engage in conversation and dialogue while avoiding the trap of attack and recrimination. When you find your assumptions about another person's intentions leaning towards the negative, stop and question those assumptions.

Inference

Inferences are conclusions based upon assumptions about something. If a man steps out of a shadow towards you with a knife in a raised hand, you'll likely infer he means to harm you. If a tethered dog wags its tail as you approach it, you'll probably infer that it is friendly. Inferences may or may not be accurate, logical, or justified.

Situation Two	Situation Two
Situation: A person is lying in the gutter.	Situation: A person is lying in the gutter.
Assumption:	Assumption:
Bums lie in gutters	People don't lie in gutters
Inference:	Inference:
That person is a bum.	That person may need help.

We automatically make inferences on our assumptions about what's going on around us. It happens quickly. We see dark clouds and infer it'll rain. We hear a car drive up and infer that the taxi we called has arrived. We see a neighbor smiling and infer she is happy. If your son is late, you think he is being defiant. You see a tall guy in a baseball uniform and you think he must be a pretty good ballplayer.

Fallacy

A fallacy is an error in reasoning resulting in a misconception, rendering an argument invalid. Fallacious ploys like those below can be used to win arguments regardless of their merits.

Common Fallacies

Ad hominen, which literally means "to the man," is an attack that ignores the argument to criticize the person making the point instead. Examples include: "You are a Republican. Everyone knows you're out for the rich." "You are only a secretary, so you can't understand finance."

Circular Argument, also know as begging the question, assumes what it is trying to prove. It is a discussion in which one uses the conclusion as a premise—that is, when the person makes a conclusion based on material that has already been assumed in the argument. Examples include: "Mayor Jones is a great communicator because he has the knack of talking effectively to people." "You can't give me a C. I'm an A student!"

False Correlation assumes causality when none exists just because two actions occur at the same time or otherwise seem related. Examples include:

"When it rains, I get sick. Therefore, the rain causes illness." "It's dark so it must be dangerous out there."

False Dichotomy creates an either/or situation when there are more than two alternatives. Examples include: "Would you like to cut the grass today or tomorrow?" "Do you beat your wife or just yell at her when you're angry?"

Guilt by Association involves making negative judgments about people or their arguments based solely on their relationship with others. This fallacy is a variation on the *ad hominem* fallacy. Examples include: "Hitler liked Wagner's music. Therefore Wagner's music should be banned." "Your friend stole from me so I don't trust you."

A *Red Herring* is a fallacy in which an irrelevant topic is presented in order to divert attention from the original issue. The basic idea is to "win" an argument by leading attention away from the argument and to another topic. Examples include: "Unemployment may be 8.2% but the most important election issue is capital-gains taxes, which let the rich shelter money instead of creating jobs." "I don't know if girls should wait until marriage for sex, but I definitely feel that prostitution should be legal to reduce STDs."

A *Double Standard* is a set of rules or standards that have different provisions for one person or group of people than for another. Examples include: "Men will be men, but a woman senator who 'cheats' should be impeached." "I am older than you; those rules apply to your generation."

Straw Man Argument is a fallacy based on misrepresentation of an opponent's position. The challenger replaces a proposition with a superficially similar yet unequivalent proposition (the "straw man"), then refutes it, without ever having actually refuted the original position. Examples include: "She is a bad parent because her cooking is terrible." (Her cooking may be bad, but that is not the only element of being a good or bad parent.) "We shouldn't spend more money helping the poor—handouts humiliate people and ruin their work ethic." (Spending more money is not equivalent to giving people handouts— the money could go for job training, for example.)

Everyone Agrees is a fallacy that assumes that consensus—everyone agreeing—makes something true or real. In an argument, it is used to pressure you to agree because others do. Examples include: "The majority of people like Fox. Therefore, Fox is good." "Why do you watch Fox when everyone knows that Fox lies?"

Appeal to Tradition is a fallacy that assumes that because something was done or believed in the past, it is true or should be repeated today—that you should accept something because it has been done or believed for a long time. Examples include: "We've always done it this way and that makes it right." "You're black, and blacks always vote for Democrats."

Fallacies are often put forth as shorthand ways of winning arguments. Fallacies make those who advance them seem relaxed and sure of themselves so that someone who speaks up about the fallacy may seem to be intellectually inferior. However, pointing out fallacies, and showing where they go wrong, can earn you respect—provided that you do so with courtesy and thoughtfulness, not a kneejerk negative response.

Stereotypes

Stereotypes are popular beliefs about specific groups of individuals. Stereotypes are assumptions about qualities of individuals based upon their race, nationality, sexual orientation, or other superficial characteristics. Like other assumptions, stereotypes have a way of coloring our perceptions. It's natural. Automatic or unconscious stereotyping is something that everyone does without noticing. The independent thinker, however, notices and studies these tendencies. The problem with stereotypes is that they generalize from the specific—taking something as universally correct that may be true of an individual, or even of many individuals, but is not true of every individual. They therefore prevent people from considering others as human beings; instead, they become members of a group and can be dismissed more lightly.

For example, "Union members always support Democrats." Is this true? The word "always" is one problem. "Members" is another. As organizations, unions have been shown to be more likely to support Democrats than Republicans. But "more likely" is not the same as "always." And not all union members support what the unions do. Some were required to join unions in order to get jobs in unionized states or industries—they may strongly disagree with what their unions do, but have no choice about belonging to them. So commenting on the politics of union members, with the assumption that they always support Democrats, is stereotyping, since you "know" how they think.

Assumptions of all kinds interfere with thinking for yourself; but assumptions are impossible to avoid. In fact, we must make assumptions in order to function in everyday life. If a bus with a certain destination arrives at a bus stop, it makes sense to assume it is going to that destination. If someone with a weapon comes at you from an alley, it is basic self-preservation to assume the person is dangerous. If you go to a doctor's office and see diplomas on the walls, it is reasonable to assume they are genuine. But even in these cases, it is helpful to think back later and realize how many assumptions you made,

Assumptions of all kinds interfere with thinking for yourself; but assumptions are impossible to avoid.

without thinking about them. Assumptions "grease the skids" of everyday life, but they can interfere with the smooth operation of our thoughts when we question authority. Indeed, authorities frequently rely on assumptions, spoken or unspoken, to be sure that people "go along to get along," that conformity is seen as the best option and that thinking for yourself appears outlandish and worthy of ostracism.

6

What Do You Value?

To think for yourself you must know what is important to you, what you care about and upon what issues you would be willing to take a stand. How you view things and what you believe emanates from your values—what holds meaning for you, what is important to you. Knowing your values is the well from which you can draw independent thinking.

An important step in this discovery process is clarifying those values. Values embody how you feel about things and what is important to you. Values are your ideals and the principles you live by. You must know what you believe and why you believe it to know when you're acting on the basis of your own beliefs and values and when you are simply going along with the way you've been told to believe by your parents, your friends, your culture.

Values are what really matter to you; they give your life meaning. They are what you find important, worthwhile, essential—what has meaning and special significance for you. Simply put, values are what you care about. They are beliefs about what is important in life and how you ought to behave. Values serve as guides to help you think for yourself, to judge what you think is right or wrong. When you know what you value, you can make choices in difficult situations. Without these personal guides, you may be ripe for manipulation and exploitation.

What Do You Care About?

It is easy to talk about values philosophically, but actually articulating your values can be surprisingly difficult. You may not have thought about what is really important to you in any systematic way. Values are your ideals, the principles you live by. They are fundamental convictions, ideals, standards or life stances that act as general guides to your actions and as reference points in making decisions and determining beliefs.

Guides

You must be clear about what your values are if you are to use them as trusted guides. When you focus on what is important to you, you can make reasoned decisions. For example, suppose family is important to you. You feel like a good person when providing for your family. Being clear on this value—the importance of family—helps you to think through tough choices. For instance, suppose on the afternoon of your son's first softball game, where he's the pitcher, a couple of friends invite you to go boating, which you love. Being clear on the importance of family helps you decide what to do. Focusing on your values brings forth what is important—being there for your son when he pitches his first game.

Your purpose is your why.

—Deborah Day

When values are unclear, it is difficult to determine what you think about issues. Values determine priorities, what is important and what isn't, what is right and what is wrong. They may be conscious or unconscious, spoken or unspoken, written or unwritten.

All of us look to what others think and do for guidance from time to time. We do this naturally. David Riesman called this being "other-directed" in his groundbreaking book on modes of conformity, *The Lonely Crowd*. If you are other-directed—one of the "sheeple"—important life choices are directed, overly influenced, by others. Sheeple follow cultural stereotypes of what they "should" care about and who they "should" be. We have all felt like sheeple at some time or other—maybe a lot of the time. When we don't match the picture of "should" expected of us, self-doubt sets in. Doubting encourages questioning, which is good. The problem with sheeple is that they ask themselves the wrong questions and look at disagreements the wrong way: "Why don't I fit in?" "If they all think that, they must be right and I'm wrong." That is, rather than questioning the validity of the consensus reality—the PC pressure they are experiencing—they question themselves. This keeps sheeple stuck in following "shoulds," thinking as they have been told they "should" think, rather than thinking for themselves.

Confused About Values

Many of us don't really know what we value. For example, many people make decisions based on what brings in the most money, even as they insist that money is not important. Remember the old adage: "Actions speak louder than words." The way you act and what you choose are more accurate revelations of your values than what you say you value.

A man must stand for something or else he'll fall for anything.

—Col. Allen West
Florida Congressman

Reading emotions helps in identifying values. Positive emotions such as joy, enthusiasm, enjoyment and satisfaction are usually associated with activities that we value. By contrast, negative emotions such as anger, hate and dissatisfaction tend to be associated with activities that conflict with our values. By studying the relationship between your emotions and your actions, you can clarify your values. Clarifying values is not a one-time process, because values change and evolve. Think of all the 1960s hippies who became 1980s yuppies and 2010s seniors!

Friends, family and co-workers have a tremendous impact on our values. Owen, for example, prided himself on valuing thrift and saving. He was thrilled when Sally, who was very pretty and popular, invited him to have a couple of beers after work. Owen was quite taken with Sally because she was so vivacious. He couldn't believe that she actually liked him. Without realizing it, Owen assumed Sally's values, little by little. Owen became a "slick dresser," bought a "sexy" car—yellow, of course—and started buying Sally expensive, frivolous gifts. Why not? What is money for, anyway, but to spend? He forgot all about his commitment to save money to buy a house and save for retirement.

> *Your beliefs become your thoughts,*
> *Your thoughts become your words,*
> *Your words become your actions,*
> *Your actions become your habits,*
> *Your habits become your values,*
> *Your values become your destiny.*
>
> —Mahatma Gandhi

Reviewing your values is a tremendous aid in thinking for yourself and making decisions. It is difficult to know what is most important when your values are unclear. You must identify your values before you can call on them for guidance. When your values are in conflict, choosing is hard, because

To think for yourself, you must know what you want, what you value; and this involves questioning your inner authority. all your values cannot be satisfied. For example, you may value both luxury and thrift, which tend to be in conflict. Some decisions may force you to choose between these two values. Maybe you value attention and personal recognition, but also modesty and being low-profile. This apparent conflict is bound to cause problems if you have not prioritized what is important to you.

How to Identify Values

Could you make a list of your values right now? It's easy to feel confused as to what you really care about. To think for yourself, you must know what you want, what you value; and this involves questioning your inner authority, the apparent values that come from your parents, peers or society. The best place to start is with feelings—what feels good. Generally, an idea or activity is enjoyable when it is consonant with what is important to you. Use this principle to discover your values. The value-discovery process is an introspective one in which you relive positive or negative experiences while studying how they made you feel, then try to isolate the specific factors that triggered those feelings. What you discover are clues to your values. After doing this with several experiences, look for patterns and themes in the clues. These patterns reveal your values.

Relive What You Love Doing

Begin by studying things you really love doing to uncover what you love about them. Try this now. Write down 20 things you really love doing on a piece of paper. You might begin with work-related activities you enjoy, then list recreational, social, and family pastimes that bring you great satisfaction. Do this quickly, writing down the first examples that come to mind. Include anything that makes you happy, that is fun, that feels good.

Values are not always obvious. What is really important may not always be readily apparent. Values may conflict with one another. For example, having one's own surfing school sounds like a natural goal if you love surfing and have been a beach bum all your life, traveling around the world surfing the biggest waves. But maybe not! If what you really love about being a surfer is the vagabond lifestyle, then the picture of running a school could be repellent because, even though you can surf every day and hang out with beach bums, you'll be tied down, doing bookkeeping, supervising employees, and worrying about the bottom line—hardly a vagabond lifestyle.

To uncover your values and what is meaningful to you, examine your experiences, the things that you love to do. Start with the first item on your list of 20 things you love doing, and mentally relive a time when you were doing it. Do this quickly so that you tap into feelings and stay away from what you think you "should" or "shouldn't" love doing.

Tell me what you pay attention to and I will tell you who you are.

—Jose Ortega y Gasset

Close your eyes and bring the time when you were doing the thing you love into your mind's eye. Think of your imagination as a mental theater where you can watch a movie. When you close your eyes, the "viewing screen" is on the inside of your eyelids or the backside of your forehead. Project the memory of you doing what you love to do onto the viewing screen and rerun it. Then project yourself into the scene as you relive it. Make it as vivid as possible. Some people can actually "see" the memory, as in a dream. If you can, that is good. If you can't, imagine what it would be like if you could see it. The important thing is to put yourself into the memory. Just enjoy reliving the memory of doing what you love.

Notice how you feel. Using a rating scale where 1 represents very low pleasure and 10 represents very high pleasure, rate how you felt when reliving the first activity on your list. Record the rating next to the activity on your list of things you love doing.

Be careful that you don't rate activities as you "should" rate them. Instead, notice how your heart responds. Does it resonate? Do you flow with it? How do you feel while reliving an activity you love doing? Repeat this process with each item on your list of things you love to do. Take your time. Relax by taking several deep breaths between items to clear your mind.

Clarify the Value

About the first activity on your list of things you love doing, ask yourself, "What do I love about this?" "What about this really matters to me?" Don't try to force an answer. Instead, quiet your mind and allow your intuition to speak to you. Be receptive and notice what thoughts occur and what images come to mind. When an image appears, ask of it, "What do I love about this?" "What about this really matters to me?" Dig below the surface. Continue asking, "What do I love about this?" of the thoughts and images that come until you feel you've found what is most meaningful about the activity—that you've gotten to the core. What do these images and thoughts have in common? Where is the spirit?

Values aren't always obvious. For example, Ralph loved jogging with friends. An onlooker might assume that physical exercise was what Ralph loved. But when he asked, "What do I love about this?" he answered, "Striving toward a goal with friends, being part of a team." Asking what he loved about that, Ralph answered, "The feeling of esprit de corps." Continue probing until you get to the root value. For Ralph, it might be taking on a challenge with a team, for example. Repeat this exercise with the other activities that you love doing. Make sure to jot down notes from each answer.

Activities that you love doing hold clues to your values. As another example, Tamara loves working in the community pottery center and goes there every chance she gets. It

Activities that you love doing hold clues to your values.

would be easy to assume that she values creativity or working with her hands. But when she probed what she loved about working at the center she discovered that, although she enjoyed creating with her hands, what was most satisfying were the intellectual and political debates she had with the other potters. It takes a bit of detective work and a lot of persistence to root out the values satisfied by an activity you love doing. The activity itself is not always what brings you the pleasure, as in Tamara's case.

Make It Fun

You might try this process with a good friend, spouse or sibling—if you're fortunate enough to have someone you are close to. You could each take turns in describing something you love doing and then telling one another what you love about it. This would be particularly fascinating if you were both telling what you loved about the same experience. You could uncover how your values are attuned and where they are contrasted. It is likely this would strengthen your relationship while encouraging you both to be independent thinkers and to support one another in thinking for yourselves. As we'll discuss, groupthink is in; independent thinking is out. Thinking for yourself may meet with resistance and ridicule meant to pressure you back into sheeplehood. So having a friendship where you each support the other's independent thinking is beneficial. Give the "What do I love?" exercise a try with a good friend. You may be pleased by the outcome. If you do it with a mate, it may bring you closer together.

Look for Patterns and Surprises

After you've gone through the questioning process with several activities that you love doing, review the notes, looking for patterns. These patterns provide a picture of what is important to you. Review the clues. This is where it helps to have written the clues down so that you can read them over, looking for patterns. Don't rush through this; muse upon it. What common threads do you find? How do the clues fit together? What doesn't fit? What surprises are there? Use your intuition to see patterns. Write your observations down in your notebook.

Articulate Your Values

Review the patterns you have discovered. What do they reveal about your values? Describe who you are by weaving the patterns and surprises into a brief story. Use phrases like, "I enjoy," "I value," "_____ is important to me," "I derive meaning from _____." Write this story down in your notebook, so that you can come back to it whenever you feel like it. Identifying your values helps you be clear about what matters to you. This understanding of yourself is an essential prerequisite to being able to think for yourself.

Touchstones

Values are a kind of touchstone you carry in your pocket. When figuring out what you think about something, imagine reaching into your pocket and touching your stone—your value. This is another way of being mindful. Suppose you value self-reliance and your son asks to hike in a remote area. Wondering what to do, you can touch your value, which helps you overcome your tendency to over-protect because of your worry for his safety so that you can encourage him in his adventure. Focusing on values can give you strength to speak up in the face of social pressure. If someone snickers at your opinion because it is not "PC," touch your value-stone to reassure yourself. "PC"—politically correct—has come to be identified with thinking and behaving in ways that conform to certain political persuasions. But it is worth considering the underlying "political" element of being "PC" by thinking about ways in which your personal values are in fact reflected in your political beliefs.

Values are a kind of touchstone you carry in your pocket.

7

Who Are You?

Understanding where you stand politically helps you get a handle on the ways in which you form your identity and your foundational values. But while political identity is often seen as a primary form of self-identification, it is actually only one of our identities, and not necessarily the most important one. Personal or social identity is more important to most of us, encompassing our political views along with how we fit into and interact in society.

Personal identity is derived from our personal characteristics, accomplishments and individual relationships. We also have a social identity that is formed through the groups to which we belong. We classify ourselves within various groups based on age, race, organizational affiliation, and so forth. You may be a New Yorker or a San Franciscan, for example. When traveling in foreign countries, you'll tend to feel a kinship with other New Yorkers—or San Franciscans—you happen to meet.

Of course, you're a member of multiple groups. You may be a Houstonite, a Texan and an American, for example. If you are a classics professor teaching at Stanford University, several social groups conjoin to create your social identity: classics, college professors, teachers, classics teachers, employees of Stanford, and so on.

The part of your identity that is most dominant depends upon which group you're associating with at the time. For example, a lesbian who belongs to a professional organization of architects may feel that the "gay" part of her identity is dominant when she is among other lesbians, confirming her in-group identity, whereas the architect aspect of her identity becomes dominant when she is among other architects at a professional conference.

We tend to consider groups into which we categorize ourselves as in-groups and regard people who don't fit into our group as belonging to an out-group. It is a natural tendency to view in-group members positively and to judge the out-group negatively—or at least differently.

Social groups affect us even when they're not present. Whether or not we recycle, litter the street, or evade taxes often comes down to how we see the values of particular social groups. We are influenced by how we imagine others would behave in the same situation, especially when we are unsure how to act. The higher we perceive the level of consensus about a particular matter to be, the more likely we are to be swayed by what we think others believe. We are more easily swayed when we know little about an issue.

Because of our natural tendency to identify with various social groups and to assume their values and views, groups we belong to assume authoritative power over our thoughts and actions. To think for ourselves we must question social group authority—a form of peer pressure.

Identify Your Social Groups

Of what social groups are you a member? Spend a few minutes thinking about the various social groups to which you belong—even if only casually. Take out a piece of paper or notebook and write "My Social Groups" at the top, then list your in-groups. You'll probably be surprised at how many you have on the list.

If you've ever been a part of a group, you should know when the group comes first, and when you do. You are intricately a part of both but only until you can no longer distinguish between the two individual needs. Then you have lost yourself in a conformed society.

—King Crayton

As you review your in-groups, do you find any that would typically be thought of as mutually exclusive of one another? For example, Charlie wrote "TEA Party" and "Patriot" on his list of in-groups because he attended three TEA Party protests and belonged to a patriot chat list. However, he included "medical marijuana users" among his in-groups because he was certified to use marijuana to ameliorate effects of low-grade glaucoma. Generally, we expect the views of marijuana users and those of TEA Partiers to conflict. TEA Partiers, who are considered right-wing, conservative, and pro-law enforcement, tend to look at marijuana as a drug and at the idea of medical marijuana use as a big shuck and huge risk to kids.

Yet the seemingly divergent groups have a commonality—both medical marijuana users and TEA Party members are activists fighting the system. TEA Partiers are working to change politics and government, while medical marijuana activists are working to change public attitudes and to legalize marijuana.

Stereotyping

We divide the world into "them" and "us" based on a process of putting people into social groups. Social identity theory states that the in-group will discriminate against the out-group to enhance the in-group's self-image. That is, generally in-group members look for negative traits in a competing out-group, to enhance their in-group's view of itself.

Henri Tajfel, who developed social identity theory, proposed that stereotyping—putting people into groups—is based on a normal cognitive process: the tendency to group things together, which is one element of humans being intrinsic pattern makers. So we tend to exaggerate the differences between groups and the similarities of others within our group. This social categorization is used to explain prejudicial attitudes, a "them versus us" mentality.

We adopt the identity of groups we belong to. If, for example, you are a student, you will probably adopt the identity of a student and act in the ways students typically act. Self-esteem tends to become bound up with your group memberships.

Thinking for yourself involves an understanding of group dynamics—and an ability to question group norms to determine how closely they match your own values. Think back to Charlie's TEA Party and medical-marijuana-group memberships. Why should TEA Party members oppose the use of marijuana to relieve medical symptoms attested to by doctors, and why should medical-marijuana users not consider supporting a political movement favoring less-intrusive government? There may be good reasons for the groups to be mutually exclusive, but it is only through thinking for himself and questioning the groups' authority that Charlie will discover whether such reasons exist, and whether they are valid for him in terms of his personal core values.

To question and think effectively, it is important to do so within a structure. This may seem odd—don't we think naturally, all the time? But the type of thinking that involves questioning authority requires a more-organized approach than the thinking we bring to everyday matters. Fortunately, such an approach exists and is easily learned by people thinking for themselves.

Before looking at that approach, though, it makes sense to return to political identity and see how it helps focus on your foundational values.

Where Do You Stand Politically?

We all have a political stance, notions about how the affairs of the state should be run, even if we've not thought the issues through. Most people tend to hold the same views as those of their family and friends. Do you look to the government to handle economic and social problems? Or do you believe that the private sector should solve problems? Where do you stand politically? Are you liberal? Conservative? Libertarian? Take this quiz created by David Nolan, cofounder of the Libertarian Party to find out where you stand on the Political Map.

Instructions: Read each statement and consider whether you agree or disagree with it. Circle the letter A when you agree with the statement. Circle the D when you disagree with the statement. Circle the M (for maybe) when you are unsure if you agree or disagree.

A. Personal Issues

1. Government should not censor speech, the press, media or the Internet.   A M D

2. Military service should be voluntary. There should be no draft.   A M D

3. There should be no laws regarding sex between consenting adults.   A M D

4. Laws prohibiting adult possession and use of drugs should be repealed.   A M D

5. There should be no National ID card.   A M D

B. Economic Issues

1. End "corporate welfare." No government   A   M   D
   handouts to business.

2. End government barriers to international   A   M   D
   free trade.

3. Let people control their own retirement: A   M   D
   Privatize Social Security.

4. Replace government welfare with   A   M   D
   private charity.

5. Cut taxes and government spending   A   M   D
   by 50% or more.

Scoring:

Starting with the statements under Personal Issues, count the number of A's circled and multiply that number by 20. Multiply the number of M's circled by 10; and multiply the number of D's by 0 (zero). Then, add the total of the A's, M's and D's to get your Political Issues (PI) score. Repeat the same process to obtain your Economic Issues (EI) score. (Note: for both issues, the highest possible score is 100 and the lowest is 0.)

Write your scores below:

PI score _____ Personal Issues
EI score _____ Economic Issues

Plot Your Position

Looking at the Political Map (page 72), notice the line on the bottom left just above "Personal Issues Score" going from 0 (zero) to 100. Place an "X" where your PI score falls along this line. Next, put an "X" where your

EI score lies on the line that goes from 0 (zero) to 100 on the lower-right side of the Map, just above "Economic Issues Score." Then going out from each mark, follow the grid lines until they meet. Circle this intersection point.

The intersection point is where you stand—your political position. This is not a fixed position: the quiz measures tendencies, not absolutes. Your score shows who most agrees with you in politics, and where you agree and disagree with other political philosophies.

The Political Map

For years, politics has been represented as one-dimensional, a choice between left (or liberal) and right (or conservative). Growing numbers of thinkers agree this is far too narrow a view—and excludes millions of people. The Political Map is two-dimensional, which gives a more accurate representation of the true, diverse political world.

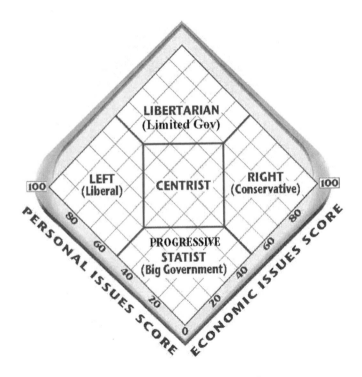

Political Philosophies

Libertarians support a great deal of liberty and freedom of choice in both personal and economic matters. They believe government's only purpose is to protect people from coercion and violence. They value individual responsibility and tolerate economic and social diversity.

Left-Liberals generally embrace feelings of choice in personal matters, but support central decision-making in economics. They want the government to help the disadvantaged in the name of fairness. Leftists tolerate social diversity, but work for what might be described as "economic equality."

Right-Conservatives favor freedom of choice on economic issues, but want official standards in personal matters. They tend to support the free market, but frequently want the government to defend the community from what they see as threats to morality or to traditional family structure.

Centrists favor selective government intervention and emphasize what they commonly describe as "practical solutions" to current problems. They tend to keep an open mind on political issues. Many centrists feel that government serves as a check on excessive liberty.

Statists want government to have a great deal of control over individuals and society. They support centralized planning, and often doubt whether liberty and freedom of choice are practical options. At the very bottom of the Political Map, left-authoritarians are usually called "socialists," while right-authoritarians are generally called "fascists."

CREDIT: The "World's Smallest Political Quiz" chart, political map, and description of political philosophies at the beginning of the chapter are based upon the work of David Nolan, cofounder of the Libertarian Party; reprinted by permission. © Advocates for Self-Government, 269 Market Place Blvd., #106, Cartersville, GA 30121-2235, 800-932-1776, Email: Quiz@TheAdvocates.org., Fax: 770-386-8373. Web: www.TheAdvocates.org.

It takes considerable knowledge just to realize the extent of your own ignorance.

—Thomas Sowell

PART TWO

THINK FOR
YOURSELF

8

What Is Thinking?

What is thinking, anyway? We do it all the time—without noticing. Thinking is defined in many ways, in terms of concepts, processes, stimuli, or cognition—and many more. In our explorations here we will consider thinking to be a kind of talking to yourself as you mull over and work though ideas, questions, and concerns to figure out where you stand and what you believe.

Thinking style is not either independent or conforming. Rather, there is a continuum from totally conforming thinking to totally independent thinking. Conforming thinkers accept—uncritically— what authorities say, rarely questioning if it really makes sense. By contrast, independent thinkers use personal observations and experiences, along with pro and con information they gather themselves, to make sense of the world. Each of us falls somewhere along the continuum from conforming to independent thinking.

Interestingly, the *Oxford English Dictionary* defines independent as "not depending on the authority of others" and "not dependent on others for forming an opinion." The definition says what independence isn't, not what it is! Independent thinkers don't depend upon authority or others, but what do independent thinkers depend upon? If you reject what your parents and teachers taught you simply because they say something is right, does that make you an independent thinker? No, of course not! That's being reactive—whatever your parents believe, you believe the opposite. You're being contrary, but not independent.

> *We should be teaching students how to think. Instead, we are teaching them what to think.*
>
> —Clement and Lochhead
> *Cognitive Process Instruction*

Independent thinking is about how you arrive at your opinions. A lot of the time, you'll arrive at the same opinion as your parents and teachers, because certain things just make a lot of sense. For example, "Don't Drink and Drive!" Aside from the risk of going to jail, driving drunk causes accidents and deaths.

The teenage boy who always challenges his father and does what he's told not to do is not independent. If his father says, "Don't Drink and Drive," he will be sure to drive plastered. He may tell himself that he's independent and "standing up to the Old Man," but he is reactive, like a knee-jerk. As independent thinking expert Sharon Presley says, "Making up your own mind is an action, not a reaction." This is where the dictionary lets us down. Determining what you think is an action, not a reaction. It is how you arrive at your opinions and views that matters, not the content of those opinions, which may (or may not) be the same as those of your parents or other authority figures.

How Independent-Thinking Are You?

The following quiz yields a quick assessment of your current level of independent thinking. The items provide an overview of what is involved in thinking for yourself.

Instructions: Think of how you make decisions and form opinions; then, for each item, using a scale from 1 to 5, rate how often the statement is true of you, with "1" being "rarely like you" and "5" being "usually like you". There are no right or wrong answers. Simply answer the way that best describes how you usually feel and act.

Openness

___1. I listen.

___2. I consider several points of view.

___3. I accept partial answers.

___4. I seek alternative explanations.

Critical Thinking

___5. I define the core issues.

___6. I am alert for bias.

___7. I resist emotional appeals.

___8. I examine the evidence.

Independence

___9. I clarify my viewpoint.

___10. I rely on my own judgment.

___11. I trust my instincts.

___12. I weigh experts' advice before accepting it.

Values

___13. I live by a personal moral code.

___14. I consider what really matters to me.

___15. I tell the truth.

___16. I do what I say I will do

Responsibility

___17. I am constantly improving myself.

___18. I don't make excuses when I act badly.

___19. I examine my motivation.

___20. I weigh consequences.

Assertiveness

__21. I say what I think.

__22. I question what I see and hear.

__23. I take divergent positions.

__24. I speak up when someone says or does something inappropriate.

Religious Openness

__25. I respect others' religious beliefs.

__26. I interpret religious edicts for myself.

__27. I explore religious views different from mine.

__28. I question the views of my religion.

Questioning Authority

__29. I follow my conscience.

__30. I speak up when people in authority do wrong.

__31. I do what makes sense, not just obey laws.

__32. I am skeptical of what people in authority say.

Scoring:

32—64: Others Think for You

You give in to others' pressures because you don't know what you want. When you sort out what matters most to you, you will be stronger. Take time to explore what really matters to you and how you see things.

65—96: Potential Independent Thinker

You have considerable potential to think independently. Exercise your mental muscles by deciding your opinion on issues. Begin by gathering diverse information, then weighing the pros and cons.

97—128: Promising Independent Thinker

Your critical thinking skills are good. You avoid stereotypes and question experts and authorities. It's important to remind yourself to use your analytical skills. Look for opportunities to practice—every day.

129—160: Outstanding Independent Thinker

Your ability to think for yourself is outstanding. You are good at seeing bamboozles and avoiding them. Be careful not to become complacent—be alert to your unquestioned assumptions.

Rate yourself now—before studying the do's and don'ts of independent thinking in the following chapters. Your score is your independent thinking baseline—where you are today, your starting score. Take the test again after you have had an opportunity to put the independent thinking techniques you learn in this book into practice, to measure your progress.

When you are surrounded by people who hold the same beliefs you do, your views are constantly reinforced until they do, indeed, feel true—real. There is no contrast, nothing to suggest questioning. Independent thinking is not a spontaneous behavior; it is learned. Independent thinkers work at it. The natural thing is not to question. So arrange experiences to nudge you into questioning your beliefs.

Break Out of Your Thinking Ruts

Disconnect from sources of conventional thinking. Mix in alternative information sources—cable, satellite radio, blogs, folks at the coffee house. Don't cut yourself off from the world, but limit the amount of conventional opinion you absorb. Experiment with various ways of perceiving the world. Seek out experiences that conflict with your perspective. Deliberately look for experiences that challenge your views. You will broaden and deepen your perspective.

Adopt a detached perspective. Step back to "watch" events in your world. Standing still from time to time gives you the opportunity to muse over beliefs. Practice wonder. Develop a habit of wondering about things. Suspend judgment, disbelieve, until you can confirm assumptions.

We are insulating ourselves from more and more opposing viewpoints— through the places we live, the way we vote, and who we turn to for news and information—and finding fewer and fewer catalysts to question our beliefs.

—Timothy Leary

Beware of Groupthink.

Groupthink is seductive, especially when you are a member of a close-knit group of people with a strong sense of loyalty. Divergent views tend to be demonized and rejected without good reason. Trust your instincts. If something doesn't feel right, even if it is in a newspaper or on a television program, question it. The media can make mistakes, and corrections rarely achieve the prominence of the original story.

Think the Unthinkable

Consider the most radical and far-fetched of possibilities. Put yourself in the mind of your competitor if you are in a competitive situation—even if it is just a discussion or debate, but much more so if it is a business or a sport. What would you do if you were he or she? If he were to think "outside the box" or even to think the "unthinkable," what might he

> *About school lessons, my father often asked if I'd learned to believe or to think.*
>
> —Ralph Nader

do? How would you respond to that? Should you make such a move first? Even if this process of thought does not lead you to adopt a new strategy, it is a useful discipline that will change the way you look at the situation and how prepared you will be mentally for the unexpected or unlikely.

9

Develop Flexible Thinking Skills

The underlying assumption of thinking for yourself is that you are a skilled thinker. But like all assumptions, it should be questioned. Certainly we all think in different ways under different circumstances. Unstructured thinking tends to be unfocused, drifting from critical thinking to neutrality to optimism and so on, without planning or strategy. Emotions, information, logic, hope, risk and creativity get mixed up so that it is hard to know what you think. Some people rely heavily upon one kind of thinking while neglecting another. When making a decision, should you heed the facts or your gut? Listening only to the facts blinds you to the emotional undercurrent of the decision. Going by gut feeling alone is risky. Too often feelings, facts and judgments get all muddled. In other cases you may be too critical, killing what is actually a good idea.

Creative thinking expert Edward de Bono uses the metaphor "put on your thinking cap" in *The Six Thinking Hats* to explain six modes of thinking. Each Hat or thinking mode employs a particular way of conceptualizing. When you understand the Hats and are skilled at using them, you can get the maximum gain from thinking. You can balance a rational approach with emotional, intuitive, creative and even pessimistic considerations, enabling you to

Problems cannot be solved by thinking within the framework in which they were created.

—Albert Einstein

make better decisions and carry on more-focused discussions.

Skilled thinkers who can switch Hats effectively can address issues from a variety of angles. When you use the thinking modes skillfully, you can better explore different perspectives on a complicated situation or challenge. Seeing things in various ways helps in making good decisions. You become more aware of multiple perspectives and can suspend judgment to try them on. Being able to effectively change the way you think provides a mechanism for switching gears so that you can better focus your thinking—like a beam—to spur creativity, improve communication and make better decisions. You will feel more confident in your conclusions, even when yours differs from others'.

The Thinking Hats

Following is a description of each Hat and how you think when wearing it. You'll notice that each has a memory association. These are images or catchphrases that capture the essence of the thinking mode, and facilitate understanding and remembering the Hats.

The White Hat

When you wear the White Hat you assume an objective mindset; the image here is of neutrality. Sergeant Friday in the 1950s television series *Dragnet* captures the essence of the White Hat when he says, "Just the facts, Ma'am. Nothing but the facts." When wearing the White Hat you are neutral and ask for facts and figures without preconceptions or emotions. Reporting only relevant information and avoiding opinions and extrapolations is the core of White Hat thinking, which involves asking questions to root out the facts, including identifying information that is absent. If in a discussion you want to come across as open-minded while side-stepping confrontation, put on your White Hat and ask for "just the facts."

BASIC QUESTION: What are the facts?

Get into the White Hat mindset by asking the basic question: "What are the facts?" Facts include quantity, quality, number, color, shape, sequences, time frames, names, objectives that must be achieved, deadlines, conditions that must be met, conditions that exist. Facts can include other people's opinions and beliefs, but your own opinions are never facts. For example, "Joe stated that he believes..." would qualify as a fact. A belief is a fact here because it is a fact that Joe believed something, even if the belief itself is incorrect. Joe's state of mind at a point in time is a fact.

Following this same logic, your own state of mind at a time in the past can be a fact, even though the opinion or belief itself is not a fact. It can be a fact that you held a certain opinion at a certain time. For example, a statement like, "When Joe said that, I felt put down," describes how you felt at a particular time, and so would classify as a fact. On the other hand, a statement like, "John was running a power trip on us," is not a fact. It is your belief about John's motives. It would be more accurate to say, "It felt as if John were running a power trip on us," which would be a fact—a fact that you felt that way at that time.

De Bono says the White Hat is probably the hardest to master, because it is difficult to separate facts and neutral information from extrapolations and preconceptions. It is easy to confuse feelings with facts because we can feel so strongly about something that it seems like a fact.

The Red Hat

When wearing the Red Hat you assume an intuitive mindset to express emotions, reactions, and preferences; the image here is of the emotional view. Red Hat thinking is concerned with values and hunches rather than logic. Inconsistency is accepted, even expected. Feelings are not rational and are often contradictory. Justifying feelings is avoided. The purpose of the Red Hat is to get to and express your instinctive gut reaction. Putting on the Red Hat in a contentious discussion can often dispel pent-up emotion and build rapport, by asking, "How does that feel?" or "Do you mean you feel . . ." because when upset people can express their feelings, they tend to calm down and feel closer to the person who encouraged them to express their feelings.

BASIC QUESTION: What's the feeling?

Red Hat thinking delves into your psyche, which is the root of your individuality and uniqueness. With the Red Hat you explore your feelings and personal responses (or those of others) to ideas and situations. Get into a Red Hat mindset by asking the question, "What's the feeling?" Feelings include physical sensations such as butterflies in the stomach, aching back, numbness, and pins and needles, as well as emotions such as anger, depression, joy and anticipation.

The problem isn't that Johnny can't read. The problem isn't even that Johnny can't think. The problem is that Johnny doesn't know what thinking is; he confuses it with feeling.

—Thomas Sowell

Another category of feelings includes hunches such as, "I bet he's late again" or "I sense that..." Also included are insights, intuitions, attractions, repulsions, beliefs (such as what feels like John's power tripping), and suspicions. Values, motives, and self-interest fall into the domain of Red Hat thinking. The most difficult aspects of wearing the Red Hat are resisting the temptation to justify the feelings you express and suppressing the desire to make feelings consistent.

The Yellow Hat

When wearing the Yellow Hat you assume a positive and optimistic mindset to probe for benefits in ideas, using logical thinking to explore feasibility; the image here is of the sun, which warms things and makes them grow. Yellow Hat thinking is supportive and nurturing, as it seeks ways to strengthen and improve ideas, to find harmony. Looking for alternatives or ways to change an idea is avoided when wearing the Yellow Hat. Instead the focus is on how to make the idea happen by increasing its effectiveness and quality. In a discussion, especially when it is about differing views about something, you can avoid confrontation and encourage the speaker by donning the Yellow Hat. Use comments, like "Humm, that's an interesting way of viewing it." Or "How would you implement that?" Comments such as these are encouraging and supportive, but don't mean you agree with the views expressed. After all, as an independent thinker you can explore and appreciate differing views. There's no need to argue with each point and challenge every statement to demonstrate your independent views.

BASIC QUESTION: What's right about this?

When wearing the Yellow Hat, you assume a supportive mindset and ask, "What's right about this?" The objective is to explore what's positive about the idea. Focus on the merits of the situation. Avoid being critical and looking for what's wrong and won't work, which is Black Hat thinking. Instead, think of ways that the idea can be improved upon. Remember to be particularly careful not to slide into thinking about problems with the idea. When wearing the Yellow Hat, your outlook is idealistic; you tune into dreams and hopes as they relate to this situation. Look for opportunities, and consider how the idea can be fleshed out and nurtured. It is when you wear the Yellow Hat that you make positive speculations and proposals.

Keeping your focus on the positive is the most difficult part of wearing the Yellow Hat, because most of us have a tendency to look for what's wrong with ideas and proposals and to avoid appearing unrealistic. When you catch yourself doing this, just remind yourself that it's okay to romanticize about what is right with the idea, since you'll explore the problems later with the Black Hat.

The Green Hat

When wearing the Green Hat, assume a creative mindset to search for alternatives and new approaches; the image here is of fertile growth. Think of ideas as stepping stones to get from here to new ways of looking at things. Green Hat thinking actively tries to escape from old ideas, sometimes by making illogical or even absurd suggestions, sometimes by exploring vague or silly ideas. When wearing the Green Hat, always avoid being judgmental or thinking about why things won't work. Green Hat thinking is creative and provocative, seeing where a thought goes. It is playful: this is the hat of thinking new thoughts. Ideas are proposed for the sake of seeing what they might mean, rather than as a final decision. Donning the Green Hat when in a discussion of differing views means suggesting ways in which various views could represent creative approaches, "outside-the-box" thinking. Be sure not to be judgmental: "We've always made our products out of steel. It would certainly make them lighter-weight if we switched to aluminum. Where would we get the aluminum?"

BASIC QUESTION: What's possible?

Get into a Green Hat mindset by asking the question, "What's possible?" Challenge your limits with "what if" questions. Turn the idea or situation into its opposite. For example, if you are thinking about a person who has wronged you, look for ways that the person is an ally, and how the supposedly wrong act is actually a benefit. Dream up preposterous alternatives, then use them to germinate new ideas, even if they seem silly. Or think about the situation from the end, and move backward in time.

Suppressing the urge to evaluate the ideas is the most difficult part of Green Hat thinking. The challenge when wearing the Green Hat is to break out of your usual way of thinking about the situation, and to use novel ways of looking at it in order to move into new territory—to get outside the box.

The Black Hat

When wearing the Black Hat, assume a judgmental mindset to evaluate how the idea compares to what has worked in the past; the image here is of caution, being the devil's advocate. Here is where you look for what's wrong and why it won't work; where you uncover risks and dangers, identify flaws, barriers and mismatches. Black Hat thinking analyzes and uses logic to criticize, while avoiding emotions. This is where negative questions are asked, but attacking and arguing are avoided.

Black Hat thinking is critical, looking for problems and mismatches. Many of us wear the Black Hat habitually, especially if we spent years in college and grad school. Many people use critical thinking when it is not appropriate, thus stopping the flow of others' ideas. Preventing inappropriate use of the Black Hat is a common obstacle and vital step to effective thinking. It's when wearing the Black Hat in discussions of differing views that you ask the hard questions—the challenging questions, "What about the cost of all of those entitlements?" Probing with critical questions can get other people's backs up because they may feel cornered and attacked. So it is a good idea to switch hats often, so as to manage the discussion effectively.

BASIC QUESTION: What's wrong with this?

You can get into a Black Hat mindset by asking the question "What's wrong with this?" to look for what is missing and what is wrong with the idea or situation. List ways this idea could fail; identify its risks and dangers. Think of ways the idea doesn't make sense. Be alert for inconsistencies and exaggerations. Point out the problems with the idea, but don't suggest solutions, which would be Yellow Hat thinking.

Most people feel pretty comfortable wearing the Black Hat. Education generally focuses on teaching us to use logic and reasoning to develop arguments and advance critiques. Once on, the Black Hat is the hardest to take off. After you see the deficits in an idea or proposal, it's hard to see the positives. For this reason, de Bono advises that you push yourself to do Yellow Hat and Green Hat thinking before moving to Black Hat criticism.

The Blue Hat

When wearing the Blue Hat, assume a detached mindset to orchestrate problem solving by defining the limits of the problem, setting the focus, determining the subject of thought, and monitoring thinking; the image here is of the sky, above everything else. Blue Hat thinking pilots projects by observing, asking the right questions at the right time and providing an overview. It is the Blue Hat mindset that summarizes, draws conclusions, structures, and controls; this is the administrative hat. The Blue Hat thinks about thinking to determine which thinking tool to use at what time for what purpose. In discussions of differing views, wearing the Blue Hat enables you to assess the direction and ambiance of the discussion and determine which hat will be most effective at any given moment.

The Blue Hat should be used at the start and end of each thinking session to set objectives, to define the route to take to get to them, to evaluate where the group has gotten to and where the thinking process is going. The Blue Hat is also a way of organizing thinking. What have we done so far? What can we do next?

BASIC QUESTION: What's the next step?

You get into a Blue Hat mindset by asking the question "What's the next step?" to assume a broader perspective—to take a strategic view in order to figure out the next step and what attitude will facilitate accomplishing it. What generalizations and conclusions can you make about the idea or situation? Consider if a particular aspect of the idea needs more thought. Analyze which questions should be asked now. It is with Blue Hat thinking that you decide which Hat to wear while doing which step. When wearing the Blue Hat, you are like the mastermind who coordinates and decides what happens when and how.

The hardest thing about the Blue Hat is remembering to wear it. It's easy to respond without stepping back to evaluate progress objectively and think strategically. Once mastered, the Blue Hat is worn simultaneously with the other Hats, so that you both act and direct your actions.

Changing Hats

We switch hats all the time without thinking about it. Sometimes we are simply reactive, especially with emotions, which is Red Hat thinking. Sometimes we believe we're wearing one Hat when we're actually wearing another. For example, you may insist you're just stating the facts (White Hat), when you're actually using facts to advance an argument (Black Hat).

Practicing changing hats helps us to become more-skilled and more-flexible thinkers. Practicing changing Hats makes us aware of the way we tend to wear one Hat, usually Black, most of the time, and helps us to be more flexible and agile in our thinking—able to call on the thinking style that is optimal for the task at hand.

One approach in practicing is to take an idea or situation and think about it while wearing the Hats, one at a time. Each Hat has a basic question, such as "What are the facts?" for the White Hat, which you can use to begin the process. One by one, imagine wearing the six Thinking Hats, put yourself into the mindset of the Hat being worn, and ask its basic question about the problem or situation. Don't

Intelligence is something we are born with. Thinking is a skill that must be learned.

—Edward de Bono

rush. Go through the process slowly, and allow your mind to mull over the question. The objective of this exercise is to learn to differentiate the mindsets that the Hats represent. Strive to maintain the mindset of the Hat you are practicing. If you catch yourself slipping into another Hat, stop and put the Hat being practiced back on.

Many people think that Black Hat thinking is superior. It can make one seem smarter to always find the flaw in an idea and thereby put an end to it. But no one style of thinking is better or worse than the others. Each has its valuable contribution. Always wearing one Hat is not being smarter. It is not being skilled. It is being stuck—stuck in a thinking rut. It would be a little like trying to use a spreadsheet program for every project, including graphic programs. Definitely not optimal. Practice changing Hats to become a skilled and sophisticated thinker. Understanding the proper use of the Hats, and learning how to change them to approach ideas in different ways, is an important part of thinking for yourself, because it helps you open your mind to new ideas, new approaches, new ways of seeing your own beliefs, values and biases—and those of others. The Hats are a tool for open-mindedness, and you appear very open-minded when you wear and switch Hats skillfully.

10

Open Your Mind

If you are like most people, you consider yourself to be open-minded and receptive to new ideas, giving them a fair review. Yet we rarely do so. Instead, our critical filters immediately engage, and we put on the Black Hat without even realizing it. We find something about the idea or experience that is dissonant in some way and then reject it—all the while telling ourselves how open we are. When confronted with a new idea, most people tend to look at how it doesn't fit their notions and reject it—even while insisting they are being open-minded. The problem is that few people have open-mindedness skills. Most people simply don't know what to do with a new idea, so they subject it to critical Black Hat thinking—as we've been taught to do.

Schools teach "critical thinking," which is generally confused with being open-minded, when actually the two employ opposite kinds of thinking. Critical thinking is not open-minded thinking. Critical thinking, as the name implies, involves being critical—looking for ways that the idea fails certain criteria. Critical thinking looks for and points out faults and defects. Critical thinking roots out ways in which an idea doesn't work. Critical thinking is wearing the Black Hat. By contrast, open-mindedness is receptive, embracing—looking for what is good about the idea and ways in which it works, ways that it fits. Open-mindedness is achieved by putting on the Yellow Hat. Critical thinking is a process of judging and rejecting, which is the opposite of open-mindedness. One of the hardest things to do is to stay open to information that does not conform to our views.

Having an open mind means being receptive to differing ideas and new experiences. The operative word is receiving—taking in of the new; looking at something without a critical filter. Open minds are curious minds. Open minds are mentally flexible and adaptive—able to entertain differing opinions without prejudice and without pouncing on them with criticism.

According to Leary, "to think for yourself you must learn to put yourself in a state of vulnerable open-mindedness to inform yourself. There are three important points in Leary's observation. First, open-mindedness is a state of vulnerability. Second, we must learn how to put ourselves in this vulnerable state. Third, we need to put ourselves into a state of open-mindedness to inform ourselves.

What Is Being Vulnerable?

To be vulnerable is to be susceptible to hurt or loss of some kind. Vulnerability is a feeling of being exposed. It is a potential for being taken advantage of or abused. Vulnerability is being fragile, weak, susceptible. Being vulnerable is threatening and unsettling. Our animal instinctual self is hard-wired to avoid vulnerability whenever possible and to conceal vulnerability when we can't avoid the threat. This is a matter of survival, of being safe, of avoiding pain and loss.

We are naturally self-protective. Who wants to get hurt? We tend to have a mistrust of others. We naturally fear unknown and uncharted waters. Change is uncomfortable and brings risks.

Uncertainty holds threats. We want to stay in our comfort zone. We want to appear to others as smart and well-informed. Unmasking our true emotions and reactions can expose us to judgments, rejection, and ridicule.

Yet as humans we have a higher self—a conscious awareness that goes beyond instinct. Sometimes we must go against the strong inclination to protect ourselves to deliberately expose ourselves to vulnerability for a purpose, such as when learning a new skill. Imagine being in training to be a forest-fire fighter who must parachute into remote forest blazes. Doing so requires overcoming natural resistance to vulnerability. And this is true of all learning.

Unfortunately, as we age, we tend to avoid vulnerability by avoiding change, so our learning opportunities are reduced and new learning slows. We've all had the experience of a reunion with an old friend, when listening to them saying how they've been, noticing how he or she has held onto some old beliefs that we discarded long ago. Probably the friend has not put herself into a state of vulnerable openness for a long time. Personal growth involves trying out new behaviors, attitudes, and beliefs. Trying out something makes us vulnerable to failure and ridicule. When learning, we make mistakes, we look foolish—even absurd. Who likes that? Willingness to take chances in life, to try new experiences, challenges or activities—even though the outcome is unsure—demands being vulnerable while doing so. Open-mindedness is one of those activities that we must do deliberately, because we are naturally inclined to avoid the vulnerability it entails.

Chaos is beautiful. Now many times we are afraid because we want order. We can't deal with the confusion and disorder. We want form. We want rules. Yes, throughout human history there have been people—religious leaders, political leaders—who will give you order. They will give you rules and commandments.

But chaos is basically good. Relax. Surf the waves of chaos and learn how to redesign your own realities. Sit back. Flow. Open your eyes. Turn off your minds. Unfocus, and let the waves of chaos roll over your brain. Float. Drift. Zoom. Design. Create new order, your order, your style from chaos.

—Timothy Leary

Leary teaches much about becoming more mentally flexible, open-minded, and creative—essential skills for independent thinkers. He urged, "Go with the flow"—don't cling to idea-structures. Change and evolve. He advised, "Be cool. Don't panic. Chaos is good. Chaos creates infinite possibilities." We live in a chaotic world that continuously changes. We can't control chaos, but can "surf the waves of chaos." It is important not to romanticize these statements, which can seem to be the essence of bumper-sticker glibness—look at them as a blueprint for flexibility in thinking, not an attempt to be glib, which was not Leary's aim.

Open-Mindedness Is a Skill

Open-mindedness is the willingness to accept new ideas "as if" true and to search actively for evidence to support an idea even when it goes against your favored beliefs, plans or goals. Open-mindedness is a style of thinking and, like thinking for yourself, is a skill that is learned and requires practice. As you become proficient in maintaining an open mind, you'll feel more confident and less vulnerable.

Open-mindedness includes a respect for the beliefs and values of others even when they conflict with our own. We are defined by our personal beliefs, so it is not surprising that we are very protective of what we believe. Being open-minded is a prerequisite to being able to formulate your own opinions. Open-mindedness helps in looking at issues from more than one perspective, giving you more options. When you give yourself more options, you're likely to find better solutions. Having an open mind helps expand your horizons, making them more diverse, interesting, and making you more capable.

When unskilled thinkers hear someone say something that they react to negatively, they respond "as if" the utterance is false and stop listening, because they put on the Black Hat and look for what must be wrong with the idea as well as with the person to account for why he or she would say something so unacceptable. Psychologist George Miller says, "In order to understand what another person is saying, you must assume that it is true and try to find out what it could be true of." When somebody says, "Hey! The government should provide everyone with a home!" an open-minded response is "Oh? How would that work?" followed by careful listening, with full attention. Listening to the person's view on government-provided housing does not mean that you agree with the idea; rather it shows that you're listening carefully to better understand the speaker's viewpoint. When others think you are genuinely working to understand their views, they tend to like and respect you more and to be more receptive to your ideas.

Do not go where the path may lead, go instead where there is no path and leave a trail.

—Ralph Waldo Emerson

Mind Closers

There are several cognitive tendencies that work against open-minded thinking. One of the most common is selective exposure: exposing ourselves to information that we already know supports our beliefs. For example, Liberals read liberal newspapers, and Conservatives read conservative newspapers. Related to selective exposure is polarization: being less critical of information that supports our beliefs than of information that refutes them. For example, Liberals list benefits of big government, while Conservatives list government abuses. A phenomenon called primary effects works against open-mindedness: information we encounter first has more impact on our opinions than does subsequent information. Trial lawyers struggle with this phenomenon, because when jurors form a belief, that belief becomes resistant to subsequently presented evidence. Be alert to these mind closers in others and also in yourself. Find ways to work against them.

Practice Open-Mindedness

The need to be "right" is a powerful mind-closer. Many people have a near obsession with "knowing" everything—being right, knowing the truth, and having the most up-to-date and accurate information. Don't be fooled by their confidence. No one is right all the time. No one has all the answers. You may have strong views of certain opinions and values that you "feel" are absolutely right. However, when you think about it, you'll realize that another person's opinions and values are always true for that person, even when they are the opposite of yours. Whatever we believe or value is true for us. It is futile to try to convince others that they are wrong and we are right. For example, suppose you prefer chocolate ice cream, while your friend prefers strawberry. Whose preference is "right"? It doesn't make any sense to argue with your friend about preferring strawberry over chocolate. Instead, you simply accept the difference in preference. It helps to think of opinions in a similar way. Your opinion is right for you and the other person's opinion is right as well. Trying to change others' views by convincing them that they are "wrong" and that you are "right" alienates them and gets you worked up and agitated. Best to cultivate an accepting, "live and let live" attitude when discussing different ideas—then friends (and foes) will see you as open-minded.

Returning to Leary's insight, he says we must learn to put ourselves in a state of vulnerable open-mindedness in order to inform ourselves. In other words, open-mindedness is a skill to be learned, a set of steps we can implement with the purpose of informing ourselves.

Put On Your Yellow Hat

Open-mindedness requires wearing the Yellow Hat. Assume a supportive and nurturing mind-set and listen for ways to strengthen and improve the idea being presented. Probe for benefits in the idea. Probing involves asking questions. Keep the operative question in mind: What's right about this idea? Focus on what works about the idea or ways to make it happen. Explore the positives. Look for the merits of the situation or idea. Remember, when thinking with an open mind, you accept the idea "as if" it is a great notion that you agree with. Avoid being critical or looking for what's wrong and won't work, which is Black Hat thinking. Tune into dreams and hopes as they relate to the idea or proposal. Look for ways to flesh out the idea. Think of positive speculations and proposals.

Being receptive and keeping your focus on the positive is the biggest challenge of open-mindedness, because most of us have a tendency to look for what's wrong, especially those of us with graduate degrees. We want to avoid appearing unrealistic and Pollyannaish. And we've been trained in school to think "critically." Find the flaw in the idea and you look smart. So we "play the devil's advocate," which involves being critical and looking for flaws. When you catch yourself doing this, switch to "playing the angel's advocate." Remind yourself that exploring what is right and workable about an idea does not mean that you agree with it. It's okay to romanticize about what is right with the idea. You'll explore the flaws in the idea—think critically about it—later, when wearing the Black Hat.

Mind-Opening Exercises

Putting yourself into new environments, especially with people who are culturally or politically different, can help loosen you up to be more intellectually flexible. Practice open-mindedness with people you meet during your day. Promote new ways of thinking about the world by doing unique, random, different, even ridiculous things. Not only does this help open your mind to new perspectives, but the increased brain activity via thinking a lot or experiencing new stimuli makes you smarter, more energetic, more creative, and more sociable. Challenge yourself. When you hear someone express a view that annoys you, stop! Deliberately put yourself into open-mindedness—put on your Yellow Hat—and look for what's right and what works about the idea. Better yet, initially assume an "as if true" attitude for your exploration.

Deliberately expose yourself to new experiences. For example, listen to music you usually ignore. Perhaps you always listen to jazz; dial up country music. Listen to a talk radio show, especially if the host has a different political bent from yours. Notice what is "interesting" even if you disagree with it. If you're left-leaning politically, listen to a conservative show. Listen mindfully; take it all in without judging. Rather than refuting and challenging the host, notice where you agree. Notice your knee-jerk tendencies while listening to views that oppose yours. You don't have to agree with ideas to hear and chew on them. Pretend that you are an anthropologist observing a foreign culture. Study the material in the show, the show's host and so forth from a detached anthropological or sociological view. Remember, listening is not agreeing. Noticing something interesting is not endorsing. It is exercising an open mind—a receptive mind.

In a similar vein, open your mind to different religious and political views. Attend meetings at different places of worship, or watch such services on TV. Visit churches, synagogues, mosques, temples. Take a controversial issue about which you have a strong opinion and make a list supporting your opinion with as much evidence and as many actual citations as possible. Then make a second list espousing the opposite view—again with evidence and citations.

When we bump up against new perspectives and experiences, when we are asked new questions that force us to think more deeply about our assumptions, we can change our minds. We don't have to — but the fact that we can is most important.

—Timothy Leary

Listen with Interest

Practice the art of listening carefully. Listening is receiving—an open mind is receptive. Listening is not agreeing; it is simply receiving. Bite your tongue when you feel like blurting out your objecting opinions. People will be more open to your views when they see that you are striving to understand theirs. A powerful way to communicate your sincere interest is to summarize your understanding of what the person has said. Start your summary with, "Let me see if I can summarize your position." Be careful not to "tell" others what they are saying, which can be off-putting when you are wrong. "Are you saying . . .?" is more effective than, "So what you are saying is . . ." – which is telling. Then end your summary with a question like, "Have I gotten it right?" or "Are there any more benefits to XYZ Health Care Program?" or "Is there anything else?" or "Is there anything I missed? or "Is that how you see it?"

What is powerful about this simple summarizing technique is that you communicate interest and understanding without agreeing. In fact, you may disagree with their view. By listening carefully, then summarizing, you can explore how another person— even an adversary—sees an issue, without getting yourself pulled into an argument. When adversaries feel you've sincerely tried to understand their view, they will be more open to considering yours. A person who acknowledges others' points of view sounds much more credible and open-minded.

As you listen to the person's view, sprinkle your listening with nods and with words and phrases such as, "Un huh," "Hummm," "I see," "That makes sense," "I see that's important to you," "Oh," "Mmm-hmm," "So you believe..," "I see where you're coming from," "That's a good point." Psychologists call this active listening. When you use active listening, you'll be delighted to discover that others find you to be a "good conversationalist" and will seek you out at social get-togethers.

Get Informed

If you know you'll be around folks with a particular view that differs from yours, do advance research. Having some basic knowledge of the controversial subject allows you to join the discussion. Informing yourself on the views of others gives you more credibility. For example, comments of a Libertarian speaking to a Progressive are likely to be taken more seriously when the Libertarian shows a thorough knowledge of the Progressive agenda, as compared to speaking from stereotypes. The multiplicity of search engines on the Internet makes it easy to do quick research on virtually any topic.

11

Tolerate Uncertainty

We humans have a great deal of trouble tolerating uncertainty because it provokes anxiety. Experiments show that more-anxious people have lower tolerance of ambiguity and are more likely to generalize and miss nuances of perception, not because they are less intelligent or less sensitive or more prejudiced, but simply because they are more anxious.

Uncertainty is ever-present in our lives. Everything is changing so quickly that stability seems an impossible dream. What can we depend upon? In the past, people's goals were determined largely by their class, gender, skin color, wealth, place of residence or other factors. There were limitations—but also a sense of firmness, of knowing where one stood and where one was going. Today, the possibilities are endless, which sounds like a good thing, but it can be unnerving, even frightening.

One of the most difficult elements of thinking for yourself involves accepting this chaos, even embracing it. Keeping your mind open requires you to be in a vulnerable state—accepting a wide variety of possible views. Struggling with simultaneous multiple self-exclusive possibilities can feel worse than having no options whatsoever. With no options, there is only one opinion—thinking for yourself is impossible— and unpleasant though the single notion may be, you must accept it. But in the total openness of a

Confusion is the beginning of wisdom.

—Socrates

multitude of possibilities, the mind has nothing firm to grasp, so it floats from possibility to possibility, idea to idea. Around and around and around, worrying, trying to figure out what to question and how to question. One of the hardest things to understand about questioning authority to think for yourself is that this uncomfortable, highly dislocating vulnerability is a good thing. By coming unmoored, your mind can drift from idea to idea, exploring the various possibilities, searching for pluses and minuses in each one, until eventually deciding where to come to rest.

The chaotic confusion that comes with being open to multiple ideas and approaches infects all thinking, and "infects" is the right word. It feels like a disease, as if your thinking—about anything and everything—is contaminated with foreign material, items that come from somewhere else and, like alien spores, are trying to turn your mind and your brain into something different. In fact, that is exactly what is happening: your mind and brain are *becoming*, but our language doesn't allow them simply to become. Your mind and brain must become something, a specific thing...become, for example, a resident of Place A or Place B or Place C, or become a person doing Job A or Job B or Job C, or a Democrat, or a Libertarian, or a Conservative, or an Independent, or...? The chaos and emotional vulnerability of thinking for yourself come from the reality of becoming without becoming anything specific.

The whole point of thinking for yourself is to consider all possibilities and perspectives, from those you already find obvious—even though they may be wrong—to those that seem completely outrageous, even though they may be correct—for others if not for you. You are not becoming something else by questioning authority, including your own internalized authority—you are simply becoming a thinker-for-yourself. Eventually your questioning will lead you to decisions about whether authority is correct, whether it is in line with your personal values to go along with what "everyone knows" or to accept some alternative approach. No matter what decisions you make, you always decide something. And if you make no decision, that is itself a decision, and you end up accepting whatever the consequence of that decisive non-decision may be. But the process of thinking for yourself before deciding what is consonant with what matters most deeply to you— or of deciding not to make a decision—is a difficult one, fraught with feelings of disconnection, of not knowing where you are going or how you are going to get there. Accepting this confusion is crucial to thinking for yourself effectively, but no one says it is easy. It requires a willingness to drift from idea to idea, without closing on a conclusion, but keeping all possibilities in the air while gathering information about them. This is quite difficult to do, because of the way our minds work.

Humans are pattern makers—in fact, it can be argued that patterning is our defining characteristic, separating us from all other animals. In working through thoughts on an issue, we evaluate possible new patterns and decide whether we fit within them and whether they match some internal mind/brain map in a way that accords with our sense of self. But using the techniques of thinking for yourself, employing the Thinking Hats to, for example, find positives even in ideas to which your first reaction is negative, means having simultaneous equal-value options—and that requires holding multiple potential patterns in your mind at the same time. It feels as if your brain is first expanding, then on the verge of exploding. Can it possibly hold all the differing scenarios, including both the ones that exclude others and the ones that overlap and encompass others?

In reality, the brain can hold all these possibilities, but the stress level associated with holding them is extremely high. The stress-hormone release in our bodies is a physical condition tied originally to response to physical danger, but today the physiological components of stress have become responses to non-physical threats. Similarly, the mind's response to conflicting multiple possibilities, all lacking a sense of necessity that would decisively push or pull in one direction rather than another, produces a sense of constant confusion, upset and "mind spinning" akin to physical dizziness and itself making it even more difficult to move in a definitive direction that would involve making a firm decision and thereby turning your back on all the other, equally valid and equally useful decision possibilities. These are not easy waves to surf. And even if no decision needs to be made—if you are simply exploring multiple scenarios in as open-minded a way as possible, using the Thinking Hats effectively—the feeling of being adrift in a sea of possibilities is a highly disturbing one.

Learn to Tolerate Uncertainty

We humans instinctively avoid uncertain situations because with uncertainty come unpredictable risks. For the vast majority of workers, a known weekly paycheck is far preferable to one that varies week to week and may not show

In questions of science, the authority of a thousand is not worth the humble reasoning of a single individual.
—Galileo

up at all—as is the case in **We humans**
commission-only sales and much **instinctively avoid**
freelance work. Could you pay **uncertain situ-**
your mortgage, buy food and **ations because**
clothing, manage credit-card **with uncertainty**
debt, if you did not know from **come unpredict-**
week to week how much money, **able risks.**
if any, you would be bringing in?
Most people would find this profoundly upsetting.

As a general rule, many people check things over
and over to reduce the feeling of uncertainty. Seeking
reassurance and asking others the same questions
repeatedly is another response. Some people cope
with uncertainty by creating lists to make sure they
do not forget. Worrying is a common reaction. You
may torment yourself with "What if ..." questions
and dwell on potential catastrophes: "What if I go
against the group on this issue? Will I be shut out
by my friends?" "What if I stand up to the boss? Will
I lose my job?" While we engage in these behaviors
to cope with the feeling of being lost and confused,
they actually increase feelings of uncertainty and
anxiety. The only antidote to uncertainty is learning
to tolerate it.

Part of Life

We have a love-hate relationship with certainty.
On the one hand, we gravitate towards activities
that bring certainty, because life is easier when it is
predictable. We know what will happen, so we can
prepare for storms and other disruptions. We feel
safer because we can prepare for potential dangers.
This is the tremendous attraction of "going along to
get along." Yet always following certainty can bring
routine and boredom. We stop paying attention and
go through life in a kind of sleep, wondering where

the time went. By contrast, coping with uncertainty keeps us awake, alert and alive. If there is one thing that is certain, it is that life is unpredictable. Anything might happen. There are dangers. We naturally strive to make life more certain, but we also take risks and try new things, and in the process we learn.

Life isn't simple and the world is not black and white. We have no crystal ball to show us the future. Uncertainty is always with us. Physicist Richard B. Feynman says, "I can live with doubt and uncertainty and not knowing. I think it is much more interesting to live not knowing than to have answers that might be wrong. If we will only allow that, as we progress, we remain unsure, we will leave opportunities for alternatives. We will not become enthusiastic for the fact, the knowledge, the absolute truth of the day, but remain always uncertain. ... In order to make progress, one must leave the door to the unknown ajar."

Hearing this from a renowned physicist—a "hard scientist" supposedly devoted to facts and absolutes—may seem surprising. But Feynman is far from the only scientist to think this way: according to Albert Einstein, "As far as the laws of mathematics refer to reality, they are not certain; and as far as they are certain, they do not refer to reality."

What accounts for this apparent disparity within the attitudes of people who explore the intricacies of reality in their day-to-day work? The answer is that certainty stultifies, while uncertainty leads in new directions, as Edward Coke has said: "Certainty is the mother of quiet and repose, and uncertainty the cause of variance and contentions."

It is natural for humans to seek "quiet and repose," but avoiding contentiousness at all costs means being among the sheeple, afraid to have attitudes or viewpoints that diverge from the mainstream. Had scientists such as Feynman and Einstein feared "variance," much of modern physics and mathematics—that is, much of our understanding of how the entire world and universe work—would have remained unknown. Feynman and Einstein are among the successors to Copernicus and Galileo, earlier scientists who risked a great deal of comfort by questioning authority and inviting contentiousness.

Focus on the Present

When we focus on the future, the stress of uncertainty increases, because there are always so many possibilities. Instead, practice being more present-focused and accepting of your current experience, even as thinking for yourself makes you profoundly uncomfortable because the questions you ask are disturbing to authority and to your own worldview. If you focus on the present rather than the future, then uncertainty about the future tends to be less bothersome.

Dog owners see the workings of present focus every day in their animal companions. Get delayed at work by a meeting that ran much longer than expected, followed by a major traffic backup caused by construction or a serious accident, so you get home hours late—and your dog has not had dinner. Regardless of the dog's hunger, you will not be met with recriminations and complaints. Instead, your pup greets you with absolute joy. Why? Because dogs live in an eternal present.

Canines' ability to live in the moment and accept whatever may be happening explains their ever-optimistic nature, but the situation for humans is more difficult and complex. Try as we may to live in the present, we are constantly weighing options for the future and considering various patterns that our life is taking or may take. Deliberately disturbing the ordinary course of everyday life by thinking for yourself makes the future even harder to assess; the risks of questioning authority loom even larger. The job went well today—what will happen tomorrow if I ask about this new policy? The company is doing well today—what if it goes out of business because of the CEO's new initiative? I have done the same job for 20 years—what if I have to find a new one because I question the harsh discipline to which my colleague was subjected? We do not think thoughts like these constantly, or even consciously, but they percolate below the surface—and thinking for yourself requires bringing sub-surface thoughts up, deliberately generating the anxiety and fear they generate, and then considering what to do, even if there is no good answer.

Because of the anxiety involved in exposing ourselves to chaos and confusion, it is easy to slip into apparent certainties that authorities offer to us. This is one of authority's most powerful ways of maintaining control. Worried about problems at your job? The union will protect you! Worried about losing your job? The government will support you while you find a new one! It is through allaying anxiety, providing answers and certainty, that authorities of all kinds prevent people from asking too many questions. Extreme examples are some organized religions, which promise eternal rewards for obedience and acceptance—and eternal torment for questioning.

So authorities give order, rules, regulation and definitions to soothe fears of the unknown and of uncertainty—and we accept those rules to avoid anxiety and confusion. Yet thinking for yourself means inviting chaos and fear into your life—a big reason it is so hard to do.

12

Think Critically

Critical thinking is a powerful tool for helping you decide if your old beliefs are sensible. It helps you examine new ideas and solve problems in reasonable ways. Critical thinking is what you do when you put on your Black Hat in order to judge the issues at hand, especially paying attention to those aspects that are fallacious, dubious, questionable, problematic or unworkable. Critical thinking involves questioning, probing, analyzing, evaluating. Critical thinking is the identification and evaluation of evidence. As a critical thinker, you use broad in-depth analysis of evidence to determine what you believe about an issue.

When thinking critically, you look at different sides of the issue, weighing the evidence and coming up with logical conclusions based on that evidence. Critical thinking looks for flaws in arguments and refutes claims that have little supporting evidence. It seeks alternative hypotheses, explanations, conclusions, plans, sources. Critical thinking endorses views justified by the information available.

Critical thinking involves being critical—judging.

Critical thinking focuses on a key aspect of the issue to identify or formulate a question; then identifies or formulates criteria for judging possible answers. Critical thinking focuses on identifying biases and assumptions, including stated reasons as well as unstated reasons, to determine relevance or irrelevance.

Steps in Critical Thinking

Define the Issue

An ambiguous idea is hard to prove or disprove, making it difficult to come to a reasonable conclusion about its validity. In order to judge a claim, you must define the issue in clear and concrete terms. Use the White Hat to get the basic facts. Avoid emotion and judgment—just gather information. "Government can boost the economy by using taxpayer money to fund specific companies." What does "boost the economy" mean? How much government money has been put into how many companies? Using the definition of "boost the economy," how successful has the approach been? For example, has total employment increased? Have tax receipts gone up enough to match or exceed the amount of taxpayer money invested? Get your definitions straight, then gather facts—without judging one way or the other—so you have information to analyze.

Examine the Evidence

The Scottish philosopher David Hulme noted that "A wise man proportions his

If I let myself believe anything on insufficient evidence, there may be no great harm done by the mere belief; it may be true after all, or I may never have occasion to exhibit it in outward acts. But I cannot help doing this great wrong towards Man, that I make myself credulous. The danger to society is not merely that it should believe wrong things, though that is great enough; but that it should become credulous, and lose the habit of testing things and inquiring into them; for then it must sink back into savagery.

—William Kingdom Clifford
The Scientific Basis of Morals

belief to the evidence." *No man really becomes* *a fool until he stops* *asking questions.* Many Americans believe that the September 11, 2001 attack on the World Trade Center was

—Charles Steinmetz

engineered by Saddam Hussein, while many Arabs believe that it was planned by the Israeli secret service. They can't both be right, but they could both be wrong. What is the evidence? It has been widely reported that millions of Americans believe that they have been abducted by aliens and, in many cases, subjected to sexual experiments by aliens on the Mother Ship. They may be right, but again, what is the evidence? Are there witnesses or photographs? Are there body marks on the 'victims'? Do they have souvenirs from the spaceship?

It is tempting to seize on evidence that confirms your view and dismiss evidence that challenges it. But accepting inadequate evidence that something is true, just because the sparse evidence happens to back up what you believe already, is a significant intellectual error—and can be a way for persons in authority to manipulate you into going along with something that seems reasonable on the surface but actually carries considerable risks.

Ask Searching Questions

Start by challenging assumptions, including yours. Don't ask one or two questions and then rush straight towards a solution. With an incomplete understanding of the problem, it is very easy to jump to wrong conclusions.

Ask open-ended questions that elicit a wide range of answers. Questions beginning with "how" and "what" pull out information. Avoid "Why" questions, because asking why tends to cause defensiveness.

Asking "why do you assume that?" may cause the other person to dig in and defend his or her assumption. Questions beginning with "what" and 'how" avoid this problem. "How did you arrive at that conclusion?" or "What are your assumptions?" convey interest without attacking. This is much less threatening and much more effective.

Good Probing Questions
1. What is your main point?
2. What do you mean by...?
3. What would be an example?
4. How does that apply to this case?
5. What are the facts?

Don't Jump to Conclusions.

While the currently available facts may suggest a particular conclusion, keep reminding yourself that other conclusions may also be possible. Further facts may support an alternative conclusion or invalidate the original one. Even when this is not the case, it is always helpful to have further, supporting evidence to shore up the original conclusion. One way to avoid jumping to conclusions is to present your possible conclusion to the other person and then ask if it is what is meant. "Do you mean that you want . . . ?" You can check out your perceptions of the person's feelings with, "Do you mean you feel . . .?" Be careful to avoid "telling" people what they mean or feel, "So you mean . . . ." and "So you feel . . . ." is telling. It may be subtle in the wording, but people are sensitive to being told how they feel and what

Who questions much, shall learn much, and retain much.

—Francis Bacon

they mean. Even if they don't correct your misunderstanding, it can be a barrier to understanding and may create unnecessary animosity. When you take care to phrase your check-out as a question, the question prompts the person to agree that you've understood, or to correct your misunderstanding.

In all affairs it's a healthy thing now and then to hang a question mark on the things you have long taken for granted.

—Bertrand Russell

Notice What's Missing

When invited to respond to material, most people confine their comments or their thinking to what they can see or hear. Political manifestos tout achievements while criticizing the opponent's policy or performance. A company's annual report puts the most favorable possible face on activities and plays down financial losses and threats from competitors. A missing period of time on a job application could mean a sabbatical traveling around the world, or it could mean a sentence in prison. Sometimes what is not mentioned is just as important as what is. You might want to ask: What arguments are missing? What sources have not been used? What is absent from this picture?

Look for the Simplest Explanation

When two or more explanations are possible, always prefer the simplest possible one, unless there are very good reasons for favoring a more complex answer. For example, the pyramids in Egypt could have been designed and constructed by the Egyptians living at

Everything should be made as simple as possible, but not simpler.

—Albert Einstein

Occam's Razor (lex parsimoniae in Latin) is the law of parsimony, economy or succinctness. It is a principle urging one to select among competing hypotheses the one that makes the fewest assumptions and thereby offers the simplest explanation of the effect.

—Wikipedia

the time of the pharaohs, or they could have been built according to plans brought to Earth by aliens. Both explanations would explain the observable phenomena, but Occam's Razor suggests that we should adopt the explanation that requires the fewest assumptions, since there is simply no need to make extra assumptions unless there is good evidence to support them.

13

Be Mindful

Questions are a tool we use to define tasks, express problems and delineate issues. Answers signal an end point, which stops thought, except when an answer generates further questions.

Thinking is driven by questions, not answers. Every intellectual field is born out of a cluster of questions to which answers are needed. Had no questions been asked by those who laid the foundation for a field—for example, physics or biology—the field would never have been developed.

This is the relationship between questioning authority and thinking for yourself. Timothy Leary made it explicit when he said, "To think for yourself, you must question authority." To think, you must question. To think through or rethink anything, you must ask questions that stimulate thought. The quality of your questions determines the quality of your thinking.

Thinking is driven by questions, not answers.

Asking good questions takes skill. It is simple enough to ask hostile or challenging ones, and they have unfortunately become an increasingly prominent part of everyday discourse. But the types of questions needed in order to question authority effectively—questions that promote thinking for yourself—are not knee-jerk, demanding, negative or antagonistic ones. They are thoughtful, genuinely designed to elicit information, and in fact are a necessary component of independent thinking.

It is the first responsibility of every citizen to question authority.

—Benjamin Franklin

Senator Jesse Helms relished his nickname "Senator No," using it to show his unrelenting opposition to policies with which he strongly disagreed. But few people identify themselves with negativity. We don't want to be thought of as naysayers—being accused of being contrary for its own sake is a powerful way for authority to quell thoughtful questioning.

Questioning authority, however, is not simply being contrary, finding objections solely to speak out against what is being said. Merely taking an opposing view is not thinking for yourself; it is reacting. Questioning just to question is mindless. Always taking a contrary position is indicative of "oppositional defiant disorder" or ODD—a kind of habitual opposition to whatever an authority says. This is a reflex—a mindless, automatic response—not thinking for yourself. Independent thinking relies on mindfulness to question authority in meaningful and productive ways.

Mindfulness is a calm, attentive awareness of the situation at hand. It is a state of active, open attention to present events—externally and internally. Begin by assuming a nonjudgmental attitude. Take in the words that the authoritative person is saying, as well as facial expressions, tone of voice—like a mental snapshot—and simultaneously notice your thoughts and feelings about the events, without judging them to be good or bad. Mindfulness is an open, taking-it-all-in awareness, without judgments and other filters.

   Mindfulness involves listening to and thoughtfully considering what other people say, taking in their biases, assumptions, inferences and fallacies as part of the "Gestalt" or whole picture, suspending judgment, and not responding emotionally. Mindfulness is a presence of mind, attention, noticing—taking in the whole of the speaker's message—a "grokking," as in, "Hmm, here's where he's coming from." Or, "This is how she sees it."

   The other side of mindfulness is awareness of your own thoughts and feelings about what is going on. Observing your reactions dispassionately—as if you were watching from afar—will help you be more clear-headed in your responses, rather than emotional, especially when the speaker's views grate on you, violate your values, or otherwise offend you. Responding reactively can leave you looking foolish, or worse. Remember that you are neither agreeing nor disagreeing with what the speaker is saying; you are observing, taking in the speaker's opinion without judgment. Simultaneously, notice how you respond to what the speaker says. What physical and emotional reactions do you notice in yourself? Just notice them, without expressing anything.

Practice Mindfulness

You can practice mindfulness anyplace, anytime, even right now, through attentive deep breathing. Simply continue what you are doing while focusing your attention on your breathing. Breathe in through your nose and out through your mouth. When breathing in, draw the air all the way down to the bottom of your belly. Focus on the sound and rhythm of your breath. Just

It is not the answer that enlightens, but the question.

—Decouvertes

notice your breathing. Doing this a few times a day will develop your mindfulness.

The essence of the independent mind lies not in what it thinks, but in how it thinks.

—Christopher Hitchens
Letters to a Young Contrarian

As your skill builds, practice mindfulness in various settings. Don't worry. No one will know. For example, you might practice mindfulness while on the phone with a client. Simply carry on the conversation as you normally would—while paying attention. Use a broad type of attention that takes in everything about your client's voice and presentation, as well as the content. Dispassionately note verbal hesitations, mumbles, throat-clearing. Don't make judgments or conclusions, or even try to remember them. Just notice. Simultaneously notice your own thoughts, feelings and sensations—dispassionately. Practice being attentive while taking it all in.

To make effective use of mindfulness, you need to ask questions, of yourself as well as others. You must stimulate your thinking with questions that lead to further questions. But how do you decide what to question, where to focus your thinking? The answer lies in determining what you consider important, based on your personal values.

Provoking Thought

Train yourself to ask probing and thoughtful questions, since the skill does not come naturally. Practice genuinely thoughtful questioning by coming up with a list of nonjudgmental queries, setting aside anything with a loaded agenda—social or political, for example—and making what could most aptly be called "philosophical" inquiries. Given that this sort of questioning is generally attributed to the Greek

philosopher Socrates and known as the Socratic
Method, it makes sense for the practice questions
to have philosophical overtones. But that does not
mean they need be dry, heavy or academic. They
can, in fact, be a great deal of fun. And they do not
all have to probe for answers—some can be designed
simply to take the mind in new directions, opening
up your thought process so you look beyond everyday,
mundane issues and think about matters from a
broader perspective. This broadening of thought is
an important foundation of thinking for yourself
rather than accepting "what everyone knows." So ask
questions whose answers nobody knows, since the
answers are unknowable. For example:

- Which is there more of, the future or the past?
- What does the mirror in a completely dark room
  reflect?
- Can you touch the wind?
- Is there more happiness or sadness in the world?
- Can you be happy and sad simultaneously?
- If you read an entire book in a store without
  buying it, are you stealing?
- If you switch pens with someone, replacing his
  with an identical one, is that stealing?
- If you pick up someone's pen by mistake and
  put it in your pocket, and then the person asks
  if you have his pen and you say no, are you
  stealing? Are you lying?
- Is black a color?
- If an old boat rots away plank by plank, and
  you replace each rotted piece of wood until
  eventually every single piece has been replaced,
  is it the same boat?

Many of these questions are unanswerable, their point being to provoke thought: there is no way to know if there is more happiness or sadness in the world. Others are answerable in ways that miss the point: as defined by physics, black is not a color but the absence of color. Some, such as the ones about pens, raise moral issues. Some are really interesting philosophically, such as the one about the boat. But the point of all the questions, from the standpoint of learning to think for yourself and question authority, is that the answers do not matter—what matters is the mental exploration process, the mind expansion, required to come up with an answer of some sort. These are sometimes called "thought-provoking" questions, and that is exactly their point: to provoke thought.

Thought-provoking questions are related to the classic Zen query, "What is the sound of one hand clapping?"—which seeks not only to provoke thought but also to create a fundamental shift in viewpoint. There is a playful element to Zen questions and to many thought-provoking ones: the idea is not to come up with "the" answer but to delve into the thinking process, feeling around in the universe of ideas, trying some on, practicing thinking, and in the process uncovering how you approach particular problems and concepts. Thought-provoking questions can have, and should have, different answers over time. If

Do not accept answers as definitive. Answers change. Questions don't. Always question those who are certain of what they are saying. Always favor the person who is tolerant enough to understand that there are no absolute answers, but there are absolute questions.

—Elie Weisel
Nobel Peace Prize laureate

you think of your current answers to these ultimately not-definitively-answerable questions as the mental equivalent of clothes you try on, then they may not fit as you grow and age: you may need to nip and tuck a little here, let a hem down or a waist out, and generally alter your mental clothing as your experience of life changes and progresses.

Mindfulness is a calm, attentive awareness of the situation at hand. It is a state of active, open attention to present events—including your own response.

It is useful to find the absurdity within thought-provoking questions and then embrace rather than discard it. For instance, "How can you touch the wind?" Well, everyone has felt the wind, so the wind can touch you. But how do you touch it? What does "touch" mean in this context anyway? How is it possible for A to touch B while B does not touch A? Again, there are no right or wrong answers here, but any answer involves expanding your thought process, making it more flexible, not simply jumping to a conclusion.

The ability to ask questions of this kind is more important than ever today, when knowledge is growing so rapidly that the capability of learning is essential to survival—mental if not physical. Yet it is precisely because knowledge is expanding so quickly, making it always more tempting to accept revealed wisdom and what "everyone knows," that the willingness and ability to think for yourself are more difficult than ever.

Since Socrates used the questioning method as a formal instructional tool, we would expect it to remain in use in educational settings today; but unfortunately this is rarely the case. Many traditional notions of education, from "teaching to the test" in elementary school to the lecture hall in college, actually discourage development of the skill of thinking for yourself, instead teaching students to accept "revealed wisdom" and to repeat back information in such a way as to be allowed to get on with the non-educational aspects of their lives. Typically, teachers teach students; but the most valuable thing a teacher can do is teach students to teach themselves. Teaching centered on the teacher tells students that they need an authority in order to learn things—a fine message to reinforce the role of authorities, but a very poor and indeed a dangerous one at a time when students' deep interaction with increasingly complex subject matter is more crucial than ever.

Teach Yourself

There are several techniques you can use to think for yourself, no matter how you were taught in school. One is the scientific method, which involves creating a "null" hypothesis—a theory about the way an experiment will turn out, or the tentative answer to a question—and then trying to disprove it. Suppose you are saving money for retirement and think you are doing pretty well, putting a little something aside from every paycheck. Choose a year in which you will retire and an amount by which you estimate your savings and investments will grow between now and then. Your null hypothesis is that this will be enough.

Now try to disprove the hypothesis. What factors would undermine your retirement plans? Perhaps the inflation rate will be higher than you plan upon. Your investments may perform poorly. Health and family issues could interrupt your regular savings. Financial planners and online retirement calculators—that is, forms of authority—can help you estimate how much money you will need to retire under a certain set of circumstances. After you think for yourself and question these authorities, you may conclude that you have to save more, plan to retire later, or adjust your lifestyle in some way—after retirement or immediately.

A related but more extreme version of the null hypothesis is the "devil's advocate" approach, which involves creating a worst-case scenario and seeing what would happen if that scenario actually came to pass. In the retirement example, what if the U.S. dollar were seriously devalued? What if the waterfront property where you plan to live is destroyed by a flood? What if the dividends paid by companies in which you have invested all stopped because all the companies decided not to pay them anymore? These thoughts may all be highly unlikely, but what if they occurred? Would your current saving-for-retirement plan still be adequate? You may decide that the answer is "no" but that these possibilities are so unlikely that you will continue with your

> *The strongest bulwark of authority is uniformity; the least divergence from it is the greatest crime.*
>
> —Emma Goldman

plan as is—and that's fine. But merely considering the extreme possibilities—thinking for yourself—will help you handle any more-likely but less-serious reversals of fortune between now and retirement.

Another way to stimulate independent thinking is by asking "naïve" or uneducated questions. These are the sorts of questions a child might ask, but ones we shy away from as adults. Embrace them instead. "Why should I save anything for retirement? I can grow vegetables and raise chickens—and sell the eggs for spending money. I won't need much when I'm old." "My parents had great health their whole lives, so why should I worry about health insurance?" Try out various possible answers to naïve questions to see where they lead you—and ask yourself the same questions again and again over time, fully expecting to come up with different answers as you gain experience and knowledge.

Refuse Shortcuts

Add to the inadequacies of much teaching today the inherent shortcuts that the human mind makes in order to process routine information—or information perceived as routine and therefore not deeply probed—and we have a recipe for producing a new generation of "sheeple." In *Thinking, Fast and Slow,* psychologist and Nobel laureate Daniel Kahneman points out the cognitive biases that make it difficult to think for ourselves: we routinely ignore evidence that contradicts our preexisting beliefs; we think anecdotally rather than statistically (widespread media attention to AIDS makes people fear dying from it, but it is not even among the top 15 causes of death in the U.S.); we are overly influenced by even brief messages unrelated to a question we are asked to consider; and we routinely exaggerate the effect of changed circumstances on our future well-being.

As Alex Lickerman, M.D., an internist and practicing Buddhist who is former director of primary care at the University of Chicago, comments, "It's amazing that we ever get anything right at all." Furthermore, it is amazing that we even know when something is right—and that is the whole point of thinking for yourself. The generally accepted opinion, with all its cognitive biases folded in, may indeed be the right one, but until you question it and come to the conclusion that it is in fact correct for you, you are not thinking for yourself.

Independent v. Original Thinking

The distinction between independent thinking and original thinking is important. It is easy to confuse the two, but they are not at all the same. C.S. Lewis had a wonderful attitude toward originality: "Even in literature and art, no man who bothers about originality will ever be original: whereas if you simply try to tell the truth (without caring twopence how often it has been told before) you will, nine times out of ten, become original without ever having noticed it." And Voltaire, another great writer and a more succinct one, put it pithily: "Originality is nothing but judicious imitation. The most original writers borrowed one from another." But in thinking for yourself, it is not necessary that you seek to be original in your conclusions—only that you come to conclusions on your own, not because authorities or other people have spoon-fed them to you.

Self-Questioning

Asking questions is the essential element of the hard work—questioning not only others but, perhaps most importantly, ourselves. Lickerman, a physician who trains other physicians, encapsulates the problem and suggests a solution: "Asking myself the next question is a technique I've found helps me reduce the influence of my cognitive biases. By slowing myself down and challenging my assumptions, holding fast to the idea that what I think is the obvious answer may not be, I often find flaws in my reasoning that weren't at first apparent. It's a laborious process, but if I want my conclusions (and therefore my actions) to have the greatest chance of being good ones, there's no other way to go. ...The key is having the attitude that the faster we come to a conclusion the more likely it is that our biases have brought us to it and therefore the more likely it is to be wrong. Once we think we have the right answer and are done thinking, we need to ask ourselves if there are any considerations we've left out, if there are entirely different ways to think about the question before us, or if the answer might not be something else entirely, even the exact opposite of the one we've accepted as true. For when we pause to question our first assumptions, they often crumble like a house without a foundation."

Lickerman goes on, "One thing that helps is maintaining a continual, healthy dose of skepticism about everything. We should be especially interested in questioning ideas everyone accepts as unquestionably true. It may require a certain amount of scorn for peer pressure, as well as a willingness to be wrong oneself—but being wrong oneself has a hidden benefit: it teaches us to cling to ideas *loosely*.

> *Responsibility to yourself means refusing to let others do your thinking, talking, and naming for you; it means learning to respect and use your own brains and instincts; hence, grappling with hard work.*
>
> —Adrienne Rich
> *Claiming an Education*

Even though we can't prevent ourselves from becoming overly attached to our own ideas, if we make a habit of remembering that everything we think may actually be wrong and fight to prevent ourselves from becoming too invested in being right, we can keep our minds open to the process of continually questioning everything. Though life may be too short to do this all the time with literally everything, it will help keep us open to doing it when we should. Because to dismiss even a modicum of doubt without exploring it fully may just be to cheat us out of discoveries that lead to improvements in our lives we hadn't imagined were possible."

14

How to Question

Questions can be asked in such a way that the person asked feels you are genuinely interested; or they can be used to box someone into your view, or, worse, to make people feel interrogated. Showing that you are listening, with nods and "uh huh's"—a process called "active listening"—builds rapport and encourages people to open up.

Technique—Repeat

This technique is very simple. Simply repeat an ambiguous word or phrase in what the person has said, with a slight inflection or rising intonation at the end of the phrase, which implies that the word or phrase is a question.

In most cases, the other person will elaborate in more-specific detail on the word or phrase that you repeated. The repeat technique helps to clarify what the person has said by getting more-specific information. Getting specific information helps you avoid the pitfall of jumping to conclusions.

Example:

Sandy: This guy has weird ideas.

Friend: Weird?

Sandy: Yeah, he says funny things.

Friend: Funny things?

Sandy: Ya know, he makes morbid jokes about everything.

Friend: Morbid jokes?

Sandy: Well, ya know, he's always predicting the worst-case scenario and then making fun of it.

Several penetrating questions were asked with only a few words. "What about him is weird?" "What is funny about what he says?" and "How are his jokes morbid?" The repeat technique communicates, "I'm listening," which builds rapport. The technique is easy to use with jargon, slang, and technical words as well. Often, people use more than one vague word or phrase in a statement. In this case, pick out the word you want clarified and repeat it. You can clarify the second ambiguous word or phrase with another technique later. You can interrupt a speaker with a repeat, and in most cases the person doesn't feel cut off.

Example:

Sally: What happened?

Susan: I was explaining the details of the report to James when he came barreling in here, shouting orders and insisting that I drop everything. So I....

Sally: Drop everything?

Susan: Yes. He wanted me to put my project aside and help him make a 5 p.m. deadline.

The repeat technique is simple and straightforward. Most of us already use it. The implicit message is, "Elaborate. I'm listening, and I want to understand what you mean by that."

Technique—Probe

A probe is an open-ended question beginning with "what," "when," "where," "who," "in what way," "under what conditions," or "how." A probe is a wonderful technique because it cannot be answered with a simple "yes" or "no." For example, if you ask, "Do you believe in public-employee unions?" the person can answer with one word, "Yes!" Such a closed question is problematic in a number of ways. Not only does it yield limited information, but it encourages you to do more and more talking. By contrast, an open-ended probe, such as "What is your view?" cannot be answered with a simple "Yes!" because it doesn't make sense. And an open question doesn't lead, either. So the beauty of the probe is that it puts pressure on the other person to talk, and you get more information.

Closed Question	Open Question
Does this interfere with your work?	What is interfering with your work?
Did he put you down?	What did he do?
Were you embarassed by what she said?	How do you feel about what she said?
Do you think his actions hurt your credibility?	How did his actions affect you?
Wasn't she on duty at that time?	Who was on duty at that time?

Another problem with closed questions is that they tend to be leading. Basically what happens with "closed" questions—questions that can be answered with yes or no—is that you guess what the person thinks or feels and then you ask if that is so. Without realizing it, the question, "Do you believe in public-employee unions?" leads the person into a frame of reference, whereas the probe, "How do you feel about public-employee unions?" is open, but does bring up the topic of public-employee unions. In the first question, you guessed that the person favors public-employee unions, then presented the question to the person in the form of a question. But he or she may have many views, or more nuanced ones than cannot be communicated by "yes" or "no." The probe, "What is your view?" doesn't presuppose supporting public-employee unions—or suggest that that is what you are expecting to hear—so it is a completely open question and a better one to employ in drawing out another person's views.

Avoid Leading Questions

A leading question is a question that leads a person to an answer or puts a particular frame of reference around the question that can influence the answer.

Learning how to ask open-ended questions that do not lead takes a lot of skill

Learning how to ask open-ended questions that do not lead takes a lot of skill and practice. However, once you "get it," gathering information from people with various views, even when they are hostile to you, becomes much easier, because you are no longer under the (self-imposed) pressure to second-guess the person's views and feelings. By using the probes that follow, you can pay more attention to what people are actually saying.

Let's look at several examples.

Example:

You: Are you looking for more responsibility?

Other: Yes, of course.

It doesn't take much moxie to conclude that you want an affirmative answer, especially if you are the person's supervisor at work or a recruiter. You don't learn much when you communicate what you want to hear. This sort of question is called "leading" because it leads the person to the answer you expect or want. Now consider a similar question restated as an open question.

Example:

You: How do you feel about more responsibility?

Other: Oh, more responsibility is very important to me.

While the question, "How do you feel about more responsibility?" is an open-ended question, it is leading nonetheless, because you put the issue of responsibility in the question, which alerts the person to your interest. So simply using a probe will not guarantee that a particular question does not lead the person. This question is an example of what can be called "putting the issue into the question." In this example, responsibility is the issue being discussed. You, and not the other person, brought up the issue of responsibility by putting it into the question. Now, consider another question:

Example:

You: What are you looking for?

Other: Job security is a big concern of mine— I've got a mortgage to pay and kids to put through school. Then I like variety in my daily activities.

This third question is an example of a skillfully used probe. The question is open-ended, so it can't be answered with a "yes" or "no." But more importantly, it doesn't alert the person to your interest in someone wanting responsibility. That is, unlike the previous question, which contained the issue of responsibility, there is no issue hidden in this question. The person's answer is more reliable, because you didn't cue him or her to the issue of responsibility.

Part of the problem with leading questions is that most of us have a tendency to second-guess people. This bad habit can be difficult to break, but once you develop a habit of using truly open questions—even when you have little or no information about the person or situation—they become much easier. You don't have to guess what a person thinks or feels— simply ask. Instead of guessing and saying, "So you think xyz," just ask, "What do you think?"

Two Powerful Questions
"What happened?"

"What did he (she) do (say)?"

Example:

Other:	Working with him is really a drag!
You:	What happened?
Other:	He's always picking on me.
You:	What did he do?
Other:	He's really insulting.
You::	What did he do?
Other:	It's the things that he says. They're uncalled for.
You:	What did he say?
Other:	He makes a lot of sexist comments.
You:	What did he say?
Other:	He calls me "Baby." Can you imagine!

These questions are powerful because you can get considerable information from a person even when you know nothing about that person or the situation. The questions are empty of issues—they are completely open. You don't reveal your views of the event, nor do you sound biased in any way.

Avoid "Why" Questions

Asking "Why?" can cause problems. "Why" asks for justification and tends to put people on the defensive. People who ask "Why?" questions, especially when they ask a lot of them, can needlessly increase the emotional pitch of an interaction—especially when views conflict.

> **"Why" asks for justification and tends to put people on the defensive.**

Out of habit or laziness, most of us ask "Why?" when we mean "What?" Perhaps we learned it during the "terrible two's" when we plagued our parents with, "Why?" "Why?" "Why?" However we picked up the habit, it can be a liability in tense situations and when talking with someone with views that differ from yours.

Example:

Poor: Why did you do that?

Better: What happened?

         What were you hoping to achieve?

Example:

Poor: Why are you always late?

Better: What's the reason for your being late?

         You were late. What happened?

Example:

Poor: Why do you say that?

Better: What do you mean?

         How did you arrive at that conclusion?

It takes effort to break the "Why?" habit, but choosing words well to ask the question you want answered is a skill. Information you get is more reliable in that you are not being fed what the speaker thinks you want to hear. You can get information without coloring things with your opinions, which is especially helpful if the discussion is "heated." Instead of asking "Why...?" ask, "What happened?" or "What did he do?" or "What did she say?"

Technique—Silence

We don't usually think of silence as a discussion tool. It seems like a contradiction. But in fact, using silence skillfully can help you draw out another person. There is something about silence that makes people uncomfortable, especially when they don't know one another well. People will usually break the silence with "small talk." It is not so much that they are interested in the small talk; it is that talking dispels the discomfort of silence.

Example:

Betty:	[Silence]
Questioner:	Was it your account?
Betty:	Yeah. [Silence]
Questioner:	Did Bill's taking the call bother you?
Betty:	Yeah. [Silence]
Questioner:	Do you think that it cost you the sale?
Betty:	Obviously! [Silence]
Questioner:	Are you angry about losing the commission?
Betty:	Of course! Wouldn't you be? [Silence]

In this example the person says very little and is silent most of the time, which seems to make the questioner uncomfortable. As a result the questioner falls into the trap of talking more and more, using leading questions. For example, there was a situation in which a teenaged boy who had committed a petty crime was supposed to meet with his probation officer twice a month. The boy was masterful at using silence. He made no statements voluntarily and answered the probation officer's questions with one word or a grunt. The boy's tactic paid off for him, because after two uncomfortable sessions the probation officer told the boy that he didn't have to come to any more counseling sessions and to call in once a month instead.

Use the discomfort of silence to your advantage. When you are silent, other people feel uncomfortable and tend to talk spontaneously.

Example:

You:	What happened?
Other:	I was video taping the protest when some guy came up behind me and spit on my camera.
You:	[Nodding] "Uh-huh."[Silence]
Other:	Well, it really pissed me off. I wanted to punch the guy.
You:	[Silent and nodding]
Other:	Fortunately I held myself back because I noticed there were two goons with bats with him.
You:	Oh?
Other:	I said nothing. Just put my camera in the case and got the hell out of there!

When to Use Silence

Silence is used most effectively when the person has been on the topic and simply winds down. There is no reason for you to jump in immediately. Instead, remain silent for several seconds. Usually the person will go on with the story where he or she left off. Silence is best used in combination with active listening techniques, such as nodding or saying "Uh huh" to communicate "Go on." On the other hand, if no one has spoken for a long while, don't add to the discomfort by prolonging the silence. Break the silence with a probe, like "What else happened?" Or "What other ideas did he write about?"

Silence is not always effective and should be avoided in certain situations. For example, using silence with an openly hostile person is generally not a good idea. The discomfort caused by silence can add to the person's hostility rather than help communications.

When you ask questions skillfully you can easily draw people out while actually listening to and thinking about what they've said. The other person feels that you've made an effort to understand him or her, which builds rapport so others are more open to your view. You can practice asking questions just about anytime and anyplace where you run into people—like the bus rider who sits next to you or some standing in line ahead of you—anyplace.

15

Confirm Understanding

Even though you may be sure you understand a person's viewpoint, it's best to play back your understanding to the person so that he or she can confirm it, add nuance to it, or say where you have gone wrong. There are several different but related ways to do this.

Technique—Check-Out

The check-out technique is used to confirm your understanding of what the person has said and helps keep you from jumping to conclusions. The trick is to identify the conclusion you've drawn or assumption you've made and then to ask, "Do you mean...[+ your conclusion]?"

Perhaps you noticed that the question, "Do you mean...." is a closed question because you want a "yes" or "no" answer. If you are correct in your conclusion, the person will say "yes" and possibly—but not necessarily—elaborate. That is, when your conclusion or assumption is correct, the check-out provides you with a confirmation. Then you can feel confident in your understanding, while at the same time you've communicated that you are making efforts to understand the person's story, which builds rapport.

When You Misunderstand

On the other hand, should your conclusion be wrong, the person will usually say "no" and then correct your

Paradoxically, you get more information when you are wrong than when you are right. misunderstanding with more-specific information. Some people feel compelled to be "correct" in their understanding of what a person has said. Don't worry about being correct; instead, strive to use the check-out technique correctly. If you've misunderstood, the person will usually correct you.

Paradoxically, when using the check-out technique, you get more information when you are wrong than when you are right. The reason is that when you use the check-out and are correct in your understanding, the person merely confirms it, perhaps with slightly more information. On the other hand, when the check-out and your understanding are incorrect, the person will almost invariably correct your misunderstanding with more-specific information. In short, using the check-out when you've misunderstood helps you build rapport because you've communicated, "I'm listening and want to make sure that I understand. Do you mean this?" and at the same time, you get more-specific information. So don't worry about being right; just strive to use the technique in the right way.

Technique—Specific Check-Out

There are three types of check-outs: specific, general, and feeling. Use the specific check-out when the person has given general information or has been vague or ambiguous, to check out specific conclusions you might draw. Using the specific check-out is a little tricky at first, but it gets easier once you get the hang of it. When the person makes generalized or ambiguous statements, identify a specific example of what the person might mean, then ask, "Do you mean [+ specific example]?"

Example:

Jose: Republicans are a bunch of fools.

Possible meanings:

> Republicans do foolish things.
>
> Republicans hold foolish ideas.
>
> Republicans vote fools into office.

William: Do you mean the Republican platform is weak?

Jose: No, the platform is solid but those elected don't stick to it. They vote just the opposite of what they promised during the election.

Notice how even though William was wrong in his check-out, it led to his getting good specific information

Technique—General Check-Out

It is easy to think that you understand what a person means when you are given a lot of details. This is a trap, because it is just as easy to misunderstand and jump to the wrong conclusion when you're given a lot of specifics as it is when the person is vague and ambiguous.

Example:

Stanley: Joanie wants entitlements and more food stamps for everyone. She thinks that everyone making over $75,000 should pay way more taxes and that poor folks should not pay a dime.

The person has given a lot of specific detail. But what is Stanley's complaint? It would be easy to jump to the conclusion that the problem is Joanie's politically progressive views. To use the general check-out correctly, first identify what the details the person has listed have in common. In this example, the common denominator might be progressive viewpoint. The second step is to present your tentative conclusion to the person with a "Do you mean" question: "Do you mean [+ general conclusion]?"

Example:

You: Do you mean that Joanie's progressive views are annoying?

Stanley: She is a bleeding heart liberal, but it's not that. It's just that she's just so impractical. Where is all of this money going to come from? She wants more entitlements, more handouts and freebies, more free this and free that. I'm sick of it!

You: Do you mean that you've got to pay for what you get, while she supports them getting everything free and you paying for it?

Stanley: Yeah! I work and I pay. They should, too.

The general check-out helps you pull out the person's general view from what at first can seem like a lot of unconnected opinions. When the person agrees with the check-out, you can feel confident in your understanding, and they usually feel you are listening and trying to understand their viewpoint.

Technique—Feeling Check-Out

The specific and general check-outs are used to verify your understanding of the content of what the person has said and to verify your understanding of the facts of the discussion. The feeling check-out, on the other hand, confirms your understanding of how the person feels about what he or she is telling you.

The first step in using a feeling check-out is to formulate a conclusion or theory about how the person feels, then to tentatively ask, "Do you mean that you feel...[+ your conclusion]?" Or, alternatively, tentatively say, "I get the feeling that...[+ your conclusion]?"

Example:

Stanley: Joanie is all over the place. She wants entitlements and more food stamps for everyone. She thinks that everyone making over $75, 000 should pay way more taxes and that poor folks should not pay a dime.

You: Do you mean that you feel alienated by Joanie's progressive viewpoint?

Stanley: No, not exactly. I just feel like I'm being cheated.

Always be tentative when checking out feelings. Don't tell people how they feel, which can be experienced as pretentious or even invasive, and often puts people on the defensive, so they get hostile. Avoid phrases like, "I hear you saying...." or "You feel..., don't you?" or "So how you feel is...." In each case, you are telling the person how he or she feels. If you are wrong, the person must correct you, but he or she may withdraw instead. It is better to say, "I get the feeling that...." or "I sense that...." or "Do you mean you feel...?"

A common error is to ask, "Do you feel...?" This question is leading, whereas *"Do you mean you feel...?"* is a feeling check-out. By asking, "Do you mean you feel...?" you emphasize that you are checking out your understanding of the feelings the person is expressing. Because this is phrased as a check-out, the person is less likely to feel psychoanalyzed, and it becomes easier to correct you if you are wrong. On the other hand, "Do you feel...(angry, resentful, overloaded, etc.)?" is a leading question, because it interjects your idea of what the person is feeling, rather than communicating that you want to confirm your perceptions of the feelings the person is projecting.

When to Use a Feeling Check-Out

The dynamics of our psyche are a personal matter. It can be distressing to have you making psychological interpretations—even if you're right. "What's really going on here is that you're still angry because you have to pay more taxes than I do" is an example of psychologizing that comes across as judgmental. It is obnoxious and should be avoided. The objective of the feeling check-out is to *check out your understanding* of how the person feels about the situation.

Technique—Review and Sum Up

The review and sum up is a summary of what the person has said, followed by a check-out. It functions like a mirror that you hold up to the person while asking whether it reflects how he or she sees the situation. The summary enhances understanding and promotes communication. You communicate to the person that you want to understand his or her view.

The review and sum up is a powerful technique with many uses. It signals how long to pursue one issue and when to move on to the next one. If you are interrupted or get distracted, you can get back on track with the review and sum up. Additionally, summarizing focuses the person's attention on the issue at hand and helps him or her to be more objective in thinking about it. And it helps you to be sure that you have understood the person's perspective.

How to Review

Briefly summarize the main points in the person's story, then ask, "Is there anything else?" "As you see it [point 1] + [point 2] + [point 3]. Is there anything else?" As alternatives, you can follow your summary with, "Do I understand you correctly?" or "Do I have your story?"

The closed question, "Is there anything else?" following the summary elicits a yes/no answer. When you have gotten the points correctly, the person will usually answer with "No," or "That's about it" or "No, that's all." The negative response is what you are looking for. It tells you that you've gotten the person's story.

Example:

You: Okay, to summarize, Janet believes that gay marriage is a right and that the states should ratify a Constitutional Amendment to guarantee that right. Is there anything else?

Lilly: No, that's it. I'm really tired of her stories about straight marriages and the Bible.

When you don't have all the information or are incorrect in your understanding, the person will answer, "Yes," to the question, "Is there anything else?" In most cases the person will then go on to correct you. In those rare cases in which the person does not correct you, you can follow up with a probe such as, "What else happened today?" or "What else is bothering you?"

Example:

You: Let me see if I understand how you see the situation. John and you each have assigned sales areas to work, but John has been calling people in your area. Recently, he took one of your major accounts to lunch and pitched him. Is there anything else?

Bob: Yes! He didn't just pitch him. He gave him a lower quote than I did. It was a below-cost quote, too.

You: Okay. So as you see it, you and John each have assigned sales areas. But John took one of your major accounts to lunch and pitched him with a below-cost quote that was lower than what you had quoted. Is there anything else?

Bob: No, that's it. What John did was simply wrong.

It is vitally important that you follow the summary with "Is there anything else?" or one of the alternative questions. If you don't, the person must be assertive and speak up to remind you of what you left out: "Wait a minute, you forgot...." Or else the person may sit back and think, "I knew she wasn't listening. She doesn't care. Why bother?"

Don't worry about remembering everything the person said. Just focus on what seem to be the main issues. Suppose you forget something in your summary. If what you left out is important to the person, he or she will usually tell you when you ask, "Is there anything else?" On the other hand, if you've forgotten something that is not particularly important to the person's argument, when you ask, "Is there anything else?" the person is likely to answer, "That's about it. You've got it." You don't have to be right or remember everything, provided you use the review and sum up correctly.

If the person responds to your summary by saying, "Yes, there's more," use a probe such as, "What else do you see as a benefit of home schooling?" and continue interviewing until the person agrees with the summary.

You'll notice that the review and sum up begins with the phrase, "As you see it." This is important. Each time you review, emphasize that this is "your view, not my opinion. This is how *you see it*. We're not talking about my perceptions or what is right or wrong. We're talking about how you see this issue."

There is an art as well as a science to questioning authority to think for yourself. You can learn these techniques by practicing them, but you still need to apply them with care and sensitivity—that is where the art comes in. It is common to believe that questioning authority is inevitably a matter of hostility, or at least of Black Hat thinking. But this need not be the case. Your purpose in the questioning is not to attack the views of others—remember that you are likely to agree with their positions a great deal of the time, after you think for yourself and work your way through to your own conclusions. Your purpose is to elicit information, to understand the reasons for certain positions, attitudes and viewpoints, to look for hidden biases, to figure out for yourself whether authorities are operating in the best interest of what you have identified as your core personal values—or not. And this applies whether the authorities are individuals—including individual experts to whom you are turning because of their expertise—or whether the authority is vested in the group itself. When thinking for yourself to question

There is an art as well as a science to questioning authority to think for yourself.

authority, it is important to understand that even an authority with greater knowledge than yours in a specific area—a doctor or accountant, for example —does not have all the answers, or not all the ones that are right for you. And a group, even when it is one to which you have a strong commitment, does not necessarily have all the right approaches, ideas and policies for you. Thinking for yourself requires understanding "expert thinking" and groupthink— how they function, what purposes they serve, and what their limitations are.

PART THREE

QUESTION
AUTHORITY

16

Question Experts

The fear of being thought stupid or naïve when questioning authority is particularly strong when we question the sorts of authorities we encounter in everyday life, such as doctors, lawyers and accountants. We specifically hire these people to help us in ways in which we cannot help ourselves. It seems wrong—and self-defeating—to choose to consult experts, pay them for their knowledge, and then question them. Furthermore, the setting in which we consult experts is intimidating: a medical office, for example, or a law firm filled with dark leather furniture and an air of importance.

The experts and authorities themselves, with their numerous framed degrees hanging above their desks, can make us feel stupid and inferior. It is easy to slide into childlike trust when sitting in the client's or patient's chair, looking at those intimidating degrees while listening to an expert's persuasive, authoritative pronouncements. But there is an important reason to get beyond any feeling of intimidation: you are employing these experts.

You're the Boss

When consulting an expert, you are paying for the person's expertise, such as when meeting with your physician for an exam, or your attorney to review the provisions of your trust, or your accountant to discuss establishing an LLC. When you are paying a fee, you are buying that person's services. For that period of time, the expert works for you—you are certainly entitled to ask questions. So make sure you understand the expert whom you've hired. Ask about anything that is unclear or that you don't understand. Don't be shy. Remember: for the duration of your consultation, this person works for you.

Prepare Questions in Advance

When preparing to meet with an expert, don't assume that you will remember all of your questions. Write your questions out beforehand so that you can go over them during the consultation. This will make you feel more confident and better able to evaluate information from the expert. Having a list of questions will help you keep the consultation focused. If you or the expert gets off track, use a question from the list to get back to the issues at hand. Tell the expert at the beginning of the consultation that you have questions that you want to discuss, so he or she will set aside time for them.

You may worry that the expert will think you are pushy and obnoxious by asking questions. But having questions you want answered is not challenging or hostile. You have hired the expert for a purpose, such as to assist you in making an investment decision. The expert works for you, and you are entitled to understand his or her comments completely. What is important is to get the information you need.

> *An expert knows all the answers—if you ask the right questions.*
>
> —Levi Strauss

Take Notes

Don't assume you will remember everything the expert says. Take notes. At the end of the consultation, you might read your notes back to the expert, asking, "Have I gotten that right?" Or, "Is there anything else?" This prompts the expert to make sure to have covered everything as well as to catch what you may have misunderstood. If the meeting may be stressful or the issues covered are complex, consider taking along a friend to take notes, to free you to focus on asking questions and understanding the expert's answers.

Clarify Jargon

Experts are known for using jargon, which can be intimidating and confusing. Clarify jargon. Here the repeat technique works well: you repeat the jargon with an inflection in your voice so it sounds like a question. Suppose your accountant says, "You need to decide if you want to expense or depreciate the carpet steamer." Repeat or echo the jargon, with a slight inflection in your voice. "Expense or depreciate?" The accountant replies, "Yes. You need to decide whether you want to deduct the expense in this tax year or depreciate, which spreads the deductions over several years." You may follow up with an open question, such as "Well, how much could I write off immediately?" Accountant: "Up to $25,000 a year." You: "Well, how do I decide which is better?" Don't be shy. Question the expert until you have a good understanding of the jargon. Also ask for written information, such as reprints of professional articles, brochures, or Web links, to read later.

Don't Be Pressured

Don't be pressured to make a decision or to agree to something if you have not fully clarified your situation. Use the feeling of being pressured as a signal to tell the expert that you must take time to mull over your options before making a commitment to anything. Take time to let your thoughts percolate for a few days.

Unthinking respect for authority is the greatest enemy of truth.

—Albert Einstein

Listen for Bias

Experts tend to present their opinions as facts, but presenting only one viewpoint is a form of bias. Get a second, even third opinion. There are usually a range of solutions and a range of prices. Let the expert you consult educate you about the issue so that you can ask more-informed questions of the next expert you consult.

Check with Others

Friends and family often think of questions you overlooked. Review what you learned from the expert with your friends and family. Do research online. Some experts will find this annoying. I recall a physician saying to me, "Yes, you are right in that. But a little knowledge can be dangerous." Some experts prefer a trusting, passive client. But remember that you are there to get information you need, not to please the expert.

Talk with others who have had experience with the issue about their views. Reference librarians, who are trained in rooting out information, can be helpful. Trust your gut response to what the expert tells you. Don't accept the expert's opinions solely because of the advanced degree hanging above the desk.

Most experts are polite, since you are paying them, after all. But some will become sarcastic or even ridicule you if you question their authority, do your own research and generally refuse to be a passive receptor of their wisdom. Ridicule can also be a consciously used technique when individuals or groups want to be dismissive of someone's questioning—discouraging you from thinking for yourself. Ridicule is one of the most potent weapons for enforcing and reinforcing groupthink, the "consensus view" that all members of a particular group are expected to endorse. If you do not know how ridicule works and how to fight it, ridicule can be highly effective at preventing questioning and challenges. An important element of thinking for yourself and questioning authority is understanding ridicule, being prepared for it, and knowing what to do if it is aimed at you. And that means understanding groupthink, the context in which ridicule is so often used and the one in which it may take real courage to think for yourself and ask probing questions.

Men in authority will always think that criticism of their policies is dangerous. They will always equate their policies with patriotism, and find criticism subversive.

—Henry Steele Commager

17

Groupthink

Yale psychologist Irving Janis showed that just about every group develops an agreed-upon view of things—a consensus reality, the "PC" or politically correct view. Any evidence to the contrary is automatically rejected without consideration, often ridiculed, and may lead to ostracism of the person presenting the un-PC data. So group members are careful not to rock the boat by disagreeing with the consensus—doing so can seriously damage their standing.

In his classic book, *Groupthink*, Janis explained how panels of experts made colossal mistakes. People on the panels, he said, worry about their personal relevance and effectiveness, and feel that if they deviate too far from the consensus, they will not be taken seriously. People compete for stature, and the ideas often just tag along. Groupthink causes groups to get locked into their course of action, unable to explore alternatives, because no one questions the established course. The more cohesive the group, the greater the compulsion of the group members to avoid creating any discord.

Studies show that when a member is assigned the role of "devil's advocate" and told to point out holes in the group's decision-making process, members are better able to resist group bias. Group leaders play a crucial role in encouraging—or crushing—dissent. Researchers showed that the best decisions made by a panel investigating new medical technologies were associated with a facilitative chairperson who encouraged participation from the group—as opposed to a chairperson who was more directive.

Groupthink is seductive. We all agree, so we must be right, right? "Important things left unsaid" are a major symptom of groupthink. Groupthink leads to people believing in the soundness of whatever proposals are promoted by the leader or the majority present. Members tend to withhold questions and ideas that conflict with the majority view, accepting that a proposal is good without carrying out any critical examination of alternatives. As groupthink becomes dominant, there is increasing suppression of deviant or creative thinking. Members self-censor: they assume that their differing thoughts are not relevant and set them aside. Much of government is run by groups, especially local government such as the Association of Bay Area Governments (ABAG) in the San Francisco Bay Area, composed of nine member counties. This group, which operates largely outside of public view, plans for urban development, considering things like enacting a vehicle millage tax (VMT). Janis' research reveals why so much of government is ineffective.

Rise in the Collective

There is a resurgence in the value of the group—the collective—over individuals who comprise it. B.K.Eakman, author of *How to Counter Group Manipulation Tactics*, observed that whether it's the workplace, a community forum, airport security, or the PTA, "team spirit"—Marxists call it "collective spirit"—is valued above individual ideas and contributions. Nobody is supposed to cry "foul" or "rock the boat." Your concern is ignored or discounted if it flies in the face of team spirit.

Groups are often run by highly trained professional manipulators—called facilitators—whose purpose is to sell you on something, while having you believe it's your own preference. Eakman says that when you're in a group with folks who "don't seem to fit," they are probably professional manipulators trained in consensus-building—getting you to buy into their groupthink, while preserving the pretense of your having participated in reaching the (predetermined) conclusion.

I guess we've all probably heard the term "groupthink" by now. It's that old herd mentality that seems to bring out the best and the worst in people. By the best, I mean that sometimes a shepherd will surface. But that's an unlikely scenario. It's usually the wolves that will surface first, and the herd will be primed and ready to follow. What we're trying to do here is break the herd before we are incapable of seeing, hearing, thinking and doing for ourselves. People who are capable of thinking for themselves will rarely be part of any herd.

—Donald Trump

Signs of Groupthink

Janis described eight symptoms of groupthink.

1. Illusion of invulnerability, which creates excessive optimism and encourages taking extreme risks.

2. Collective rationalization, so members ignore warnings and do not question their assumptions.

3. Moral superiority, so members believe in the rightness of their cause, ignoring the ethical consequences of their decisions.

4. Stereotyped views of out-groups, so that effective responses to conflicting concerns are unnecessary.

5. Direct pressure on dissenters not to express arguments against any of the group's views.

6. Illusion of unanimity, making it appear that majority views and judgments are unanimous.

7. Self-censorship, in which doubts and deviations from the perceived group consensus are not expressed.

8. Self-appointed 'mind-guards' who protect the group and the leader from information that is contradictory to the group's views and decisions.

Dissent

Studies have found that conformity can be reduced from highs of 97% on a visual judgment task to only 36% when there is an effective dissenter in the ranks. When someone disagrees, or even just vacillates, unable to decide, conformity to group norms is reduced—especially when the ambivalent one is a power person.

In matters of style, swim with the current; in matters of principle, stand like a rock.

—Thomas Jefferson

Several thinkers have argued that a healthy society needs to encourage—and protect—dissension. Certainly this is one of the reasons Americans so revere the First Amendment.

Dissenters against groupthink are easy to ignore, because people don't take them seriously. They are "loons drinking the Kool-Aid." So effective dissenters present differing views even-handedly, avoiding pointless confrontation and personal attacks. But don't think that dissent is easy. Even for the most skilled, there are many pressures that work against dissent being expressed. Groups tend to recruit those who fit in, so conformity is built in. People are uncomfortable with conflict and tend to suppress it. Dissent is easily misinterpreted as disrespect or even a personal attack. Dissenters tend to be thought of as troublemakers who should be punished and pushed out. Thinking for yourself and questioning the authority of groupthink means always being aware that just because something is popular, that doesn't mean it is correct.

Power of Groupthink

If forty million people say a foolish thing it does not become a wise one.

—W. Somerset Maugham

The classic Solomon Asch experiments revealed that the power of groupthink is so great that many people will deny the evidence of their own eyes. The study consisted of six people who were asked one at a time to look at a line and then pick the line of the same length from three options. Subjects were seated in the fifth chair, so they would hear the choices of four others before stating their choice of the correct line. What the subject didn't know was that the other five people were "confederates" working secretly for the researcher. They all purposely identified a much longer line as the same length. Asch found that 37% of the subjects selected the same wrong longer line that the five confederates chose, thereby denying evidence from their own eyes.

When Asch interviewed the subjects about what they were thinking when they selected the too-long line, many said, "I thought that they must be right," which Asch called informational conformity. Others said, "I thought, why should I make waves?" which Asch called normative conformity.

In the next trials, Asch instructed the confederate in the 3rd chair to pick the correct line. The number of subjects picking the wrong line—conforming to groupthink—dropped to 5%. In another variation, the subjects could hear the confederates' wrong choice and were instructed to write their selection secretly on a paper. Here again conformity dropped considerably.

The second trial, where one confederate chose the correct line—thereby supporting the subject's perceptions—is reminiscent of a very insightful YouTube posting called "First Follower: A Lesson in Leadership from the Dancing Guy." The video begins with a crowd of young people sitting around on the ground in a park. Then the Dancing Guy leaps up and begins dancing alone in a very animated manner. The moderator notes that what the Dancing Guy is doing is so simple that it is almost instructional. "This is key," he says. "You must be easy to follow." Then a guy—"the first follower"—leaps up to dance along with the Dancing Guy. The Dancing Guy embraces the first follower as an equal, so it's not about the leader any more—it's about "them." The first follower shows everyone else how to follow. He waves to his friends to join in. It takes guts to be the first follower. You stand out and risk ridicule. Being the first follower is a powerful form of leadership. The moderator says, "The first follower transforms a lone nut into a leader. If the leader is the flint, the first follower is the spark."

Soon a second guy leaps into the dance—"the second follower"—which is a turning point. It's proof that the first follower has done well. Now it's not a lone nut and not two nuts. Three is a crowd and a crowd is news. It is important that fence-sitters see more than the leader, because new followers follow followers, not the leader. Then two more people join in and three more immediately after them. They have momentum. As more people jump into the dance, it is no longer risky. If they were on the fence before, there is no reason for them not to join the dancing now. They won't stand out; they won't be ridiculed; they will be part of the in crowd. The stragglers join the dance because if they don't, then they will be ridiculed for sitting on the sideline and not dancing.

The important lesson of the video is that it was the first follower who transformed a lone nut into a leader. The leader gets the credit, but the first follower makes it happen. This reveals a powerful social-change strategy: be a first follower and support dissenting views put forth by others, rather than expressing those views yourself.

The important lesson of the video is that it was the first follower who transformed a lone nut into a leader. The leader gets the credit, but the first follower makes it happen.

Asch showed that when others express divergent views, pressure to conform is lessened. Of course, you can seed those views beforehand, then support the dissenter who expresses them the next day in the staff meeting, for example. In this way, you lead indirectly, as shown by the

Dancing Guy. Support the dissent, which lessens
conformity and takes much of the attention away
from yourself. The dissenters get the credit, but
you made it happen with your support of their
expressed view. This is one way of questioning, even
challenging, groupthink—a particularly insidious
form of authority.

Some authorities use specific methods to head off
challenges and defuse those that do arise. A crafty
Machiavellian one, the Delphi Technique, is worth
knowing about—you may already have experienced
it without knowing what it was or how it was being
used. Understanding the Delphi Technique is
necessary to find ways to question it and think for
yourself in group meetings.

18

Beware of Group Facilitators

If you've attended a city, county or other civil or government meeting led by "facilitators," you've probably been exposed to the Delphi Technique. Many government programs, such as land use for "sustainable development," tout "citizen involvement," which is achieved by facilitator-led informational groups for the community. In these sessions, a highly trained "change agent" or "facilitator" is brought in to lead a discussion of a controversial issue with the community affected by the issues. What participants don't know is that they are about to be manipulated into a predetermined outcome.

The facilitator hosts a meeting—in person or online—to gather input from members of the group about an issue of concern. They are led to believe that their input matters and will be factored into decisions about the issue of concern. In the course of the meeting, those who disagree with the preordained plan are segregated, ridiculed and marginalized—and this is by design—while those supporting the power broker's agenda are encouraged and praised for their "activism." What the participants don't know is that their opinions regarding the controversy have been sought solely as a manipulation to buy them off with a "feeling"—a sense of satisfaction that they are "involved" in the change and that their input matters. The entire process is a ruse to dupe those who might object into agreeing with a preordained plan by designing a charade of "participating." The actual

A "collective" mind does not exist. It is merely the sum of endless numbers of individual minds. If we have an endless number of individual minds who are weak, meek, submissive and impotent— who renounce their creative supremacy for the sake of the "whole" and accept humbly the "whole's" verdict—we don't get a collective superbrain. We get only the weak, meek, submissive and impotent collective mind.

—Ayn Rand
The Journals of Ayn Rand

purpose of the meeting and objective of the facilitator is creating the illusion of participation in the decision-making process.

When we believe an idea is our own, we tend to develop a sense of "ownership" and support it; we tend to resist, however, when we believe an idea is being foisted on us. The facilitator uses this basic human response to engender a false sense of "ownership" of a predetermined outcome by creating an illusion that attendees' input counts in the decision, when it really doesn't. The Delphi Technique is widely used to introduce government programs to community groups.

How It Works

The facilitator's first objective is to establish a good-guy/bad-guy dynamic among those participating in the group. Anyone disagreeing with the facilitator is deliberately made to appear as the "bad" guy, with the facilitator being the "good" guy. The facilitator accomplishes this by drawing out those who disagree, then making them look foolish, inept, or aggressive, which sends a strong message to the rest of the group members that they should keep quiet or get the same disagreeable treatment. When the opposition has been identified and ostracized, the facilitator becomes the "good" guy—a friend to the cooperative, agreeable group members—and the agenda and direction of the meeting are established without the group members ever realizing that they were manipulated.

The facilitator begins the process by asking participants to share their concerns about the program, project, or policy in question. While the group members "get to know each other and their concerns," the facilitator identifies those opposing the predetermined decision (the ones to be nullified) along with participants who vacillate in their views (the weak or noncommittal).

Next, the facilitator becomes "devil's advocate," donning an agitator's version of the Black Hat, and deliberately escalates tension among group members, pitting one faction against another to make a preordained viewpoint appear "sensible," while making those who oppose the plan or question the facilitator appear ridiculous, unknowledgeable, inarticulate, or dogmatic. The facilitator subtly provokes "Targets," who are usually those who oppose the prearranged decision, to become angry, causing tensions to increase; this makes everyone, especially the weak and noncommittal, quite uncomfortable. In this way, those who oppose the predetermined policy or program are shut out of the group, while remaining participants relax as the tension subsides.

The method works. Group polarization is achieved by the facilitator becoming accepted as a member of the group. Targets rarely know that they were manipulated. The facilitator puts the desired idea on the table and asks for opinions during discussion. Those participants who identify with the facilitator adopt the idea as if it were their own and then pressure the remaining group members to buy into the proposition.

Often attendees are broken up into smaller groups of seven or eight people, with each having a "break-out" facilitator. As participants discuss preset issues, the break-out facilitator employs the same tactics described above as used by the "lead" facilitator. Participants are encouraged to write their ideas and disagreements on paper—to be compiled later "for the report." But contrary to what participants are told in the "orientation," their "feedback" is not reflected in the report or considered in the decision, as they were led to believe. When participants don't see their concerns in the report, they figure their viewpoint was in the minority and thus not reflected. But was it? Did anyone read what group members wrote? Or were their comments solicited solely so they would "feel" their views mattered and that all group members were consulted—with the written suggestions being tossed into the trash?

Defusing the Delphi Technique

To stop the Delphi Technique most effectively, assemble a team of your own before the meeting, then bring your people there—having everyone arrive separately and sit in different areas. You will need a team of three or four who know the Delphi Technique, or even more when community turnout is high. Establish a plan of action before a meeting and make sure that everyone knows his or her part. When the facilitator digresses from a question, one of your team stands up and politely says: "But you didn't answer that person's question." Even if the facilitator suspects that certain group members are working together, the facilitator will not want to alienate the crowd by making accusations. Stick to this approach and often the group will catch on.

There are three "B's," or "be's," needed to fight the Delphi Technique effectively. First, be charming, courteous, and pleasant. Smile. Moderate your voice so as not to come across as belligerent or aggressive.

Second, be focused. Jot down your thoughts or questions. When facilitators are asked questions they don't want to answer by people who think for themselves, they often digress from the issue that was raised and try instead to put the questioner on the defensive. Do not fall for this tactic. Courteously bring the facilitator back to your original question. If the facilitator rephrases it so that it becomes an accusatory statement—a popular tactic—simply say, "That is not what I asked. What I asked was ..." Then repeat your question.

Third, be persistent. If putting you on the defensive doesn't work, facilitators often resort to long monologues that drag on for several minutes. During that time, the group usually forgets the question, which is the facilitator's intent. Let the facilitator finish. Then, with polite persistence, state: "But you didn't answer my question. My question was . . ." and repeat your question. Never become angry under any circumstances. Anger directed at the facilitator will immediately make the facilitator look like a victim, which defeats your purpose. Facilitators seek to make the majority of the group members like them, and to ostracize anyone who might pose a threat to the realization of their agenda.

After the meeting is over, your group members should leave separately and get together somewhere else to analyze what went right, what went wrong and why, and what needs to happen the next time. Never strategize during a meeting. A popular tactic of facilitators, if a session is meeting with resistance, is to call a recess. During the recess, the facilitator and his spotters—people who observe the crowd during the course of a meeting—watch the crowd to see who congregates where, especially those who have offered resistance. If the resistors congregate in one place, a spotter will gravitate to that group and join in the conversation, reporting what was said to the facilitator. When the meeting resumes, the facilitator will steer clear of the resistors. Do not congregate. Instead, gravitate to where the facilitators or spotters are. Stay away from your team members.

The Delphi Technique is employed by authorities seeking to quell dissent: they are organized to prevent effective questioning, so you must organize to question effectively. But as insidious as it is, the Delphi Technique is not the most hurtful one employed against people who think for themselves to question authority—in fact, its power comes from the way it appears not to be hurtful. At the opposite extreme, and used as often by individuals as by group leaders and other authority figures, is ridicule—a technique that not only ostracizes but also intends to harm the target's self-image, diminishing a questioner's stature to such a degree that others cannot take the questioner or the questions seriously. If you think for yourself, you will at some point be exposed to ridicule. Knowing how it works and how to counter it is a crucial element of questioning authority.

The above material was derived from public domain information supplied by freedomforceinternational.org. There is much at this site that fuels independent thinking.

19

Ridicule
The Most Potent Weapon

As bad as it feels to be thought stupid or naïve, it feels even worse to be mocked and laughed at—whether in your face or behind your back. This is precisely the feeling that ridicule seeks to evoke, which is why it is such a potent technique for quelling questioning. Ridicule does it all: it makes people feel small, stupid, isolated, unworthy of serious attention, looked down on, unworthy of being taken seriously.

Saul Alinsky, in his classic, *Rules for Radicals*, noted, "Ridicule is man's most potent weapon." Avoiding ridicule lies at the heart of the effectiveness of peer pressure and groupthink in pressuring us into accepting certain views. When we voice an opinion that is outside so-called political correctness, contrary to prevailing views of the consensus reality of the group at hand, an invisible but nonetheless powerful process sets in to pressure us back into acceptable-to-the-group opinions and behavior.

Scorn, derision, and teasing are the tools of ridicule. Ridicule uses derision to mock and make fun of you and your opinions. You are made the subject of laughter and teasing. The intent is to belittle you in order to make you and your ideas appear stupid, irrelevant, and outside of the mainstream—

Ridicule uses derision to mock and make fun of you and your opinions.

> *No God and no religion can survive ridicule. No political church, no nobility, no royalty or other fraud, can face ridicule in a fair field, and live.*
> —Mark Twain

to evoke contemptuous laughter at and feelings toward you and your views.

As Alinksy noted, ridicule "infuriates the opposition, who then react to [the ridiculer's] advantage." The tactic is to demean and mock you and your opinion. The curious thing is that the persons engaging in the ridicule are often unaware of what they are doing. It is a kind of group-pressure knee-jerk response. Think of it as the long arm of socialization giving you a strong nudge—perhaps even a shove—back into the groupthink fold. Consider Jeff's experience. "I told a colleague, Rick, whom I knew casually, that I no longer supported the Democrats' agenda. I said nothing else—not why I felt that way or what I did support. Rick slapped his leg and, with an exaggerated laugh and scandalized voice, accused me of being a Republican and of supporting things he associated with that political persuasion, such as war and unchecked oil drilling, which sounded criminal from the way he spoke—all the while continuing a stilted laugh, while slapping his leg and shaking his head incredulously."

This is classic ridicule—Jeff was demeaned and made fun of for revealing that he held views divergent from the prevailing liberal agenda. Rick "accused" Jeff of "being a Republican" when in reality he could be a Libertarian, Independent or Green—or even a Marxist. Rick was not concerned about facts—his ridicule turned Jeff into an outcast unworthy of serious consideration, and dismissed him because he strayed from accepted liberal views.

Social Control

Scorn, ridicule and contempt are powerful social controls. Scorning, belittling, showing contempt and shaming are very effective in pressuring folks to shut up and get back into the accepted fold. The suffering that rejection and ostracism arouse causes us to give in.

The power of rejection and exclusion evolved for a purpose. The group was necessary for survival in tribal life. A strong desire for inclusion was necessary to hold the group together. To this day, when tribal cohesion for survival is no longer a necessity in urbanized societies, we still experience a sense of happiness and feelings of belonging when "in the fold." Membership brings protection, support and, consequently, feelings of being respected, intelligent and "with-it." At an extreme in modern urban society are gangs, with their vicious initiation rituals and violent everyday activities. These cement group loyalty and make gang members feel they are protected and cared for—they will survive in the "urban jungle." By contrast, being excluded brings profound feelings of aloneness and unhappiness. And ridicule, although not a physically violent form of attack, is a mentally violent one that ostracizes, excludes and dehumanizes in

It should be remembered that you can threaten the enemy and get away with it... You can insult and annoy him, but the one thing that is unforgivable and that is certain to get him to react is to laugh at him. This causes irrational anger.

—Saul Alinsky

its own way just as surely as physical violence does on the "mean streets."

When someone expresses an unacceptable idea, unwitting knee-jerk socializers may engage in prolonged and exaggerated laughter. When you venture outside of accepted consensus views, self-appointed controllers will mock you by picking on real or imagined defects, physical blemishes, or mistakes. They will deride you, trying to implant feelings of shame, while twisting your views.

Mockers portray the mocked as small and somehow inferior for out-of-the-group thinking. They look for weaknesses and recast a person's positive attributes as defects. For example, in a school environment, a tall teenaged girl may be likened to a giraffe, using "raffie" as a demeaning nickname. Conscientious, hard-working students may be belittled with negative nicknames to ridicule their success, such as calling them "bookworms" or "geeks."

Mockery is common is the workplace. Supervisors may mock how their underlings do their jobs. Adult mockery is usually more veiled than schoolyard mocking. Ridicule may be communicated nonverbally, through facial reactions, belittling behavior, and mocking glances. Speaking while looking away from the person addressed, refusing to answer, acting as though they've not heard the person being mocked, and casting ironic glances at co-mockers are common methods of ridicule. And they are hard to speak to, because when you try to describe the way in which you are being scorned, you get put down as being "paranoid" and "overly sensitive."

Workplace rivals often mock one another, trying to ensnare others with a litany of the rival's failings and mistakes. They may attempt to demean by ridiculing physical defects, choice of clothes, manner of walking, or other personal characteristics. Rivals may try to crush one another with verbal needling and belittling glances.

With irrational anger come uncontrolled reactions, reactions that make you look and feel foolish. You blow your cool, which is, of course, what your adversary wants. "The real action is in the enemy's reaction," Alinsky observes. "The enemy, properly goaded and guided in his reaction, will be your major strength."

Recognizing Ridicule

The emotional messages are carried not only by the words themselves, but also by the tunes we set our words to. A sequence of English words can be said in a way that is hostile and brutal, or a way that expresses endearment, friendliness and a loving attitude. There is an amusing example of this, literally set to a tune, in Gilbert and Sullivan's operetta, *Patience*, when a character who has never been in love talks about a childhood playmate, saying, "*He* was a little boy." Her friend comments, "He *was* a little boy!" The first girl emphasizes, "He was a *little* boy!" And her friend replies, "He was a little *boy.*"

Far less amusingly, we have all encountered a comment such as, "Oh, that's a great idea," said in a way that negates the words themselves: "Oh, that's a *great* idea." Listening to the way things are said, not just to the words themselves, is a good way to recognize ridicule. It is also a way to disarm it, by deliberately ignoring the tone being used. "Oh, that's a *great* idea." "Thanks. Nest time I think we should do next."

Forms of Ridicule

Name calling is easily recognized. "You're a disgusting homophobe." "You're a racist." "You're a poor-people-hating rich person." "You're anti-Semitic." "You hate Muslims!" It helps to remember the child's admonition: Sticks and stones can break my bones, but names will never hurt me. But you also have to consider that, among adults, names can hurt. Being accused of racism, however wrongly, could cause you to be ostracized and lead people to ignore what you may say—even if you say nothing about race— because a racist does not deserve a fair hearing on any subject. This is exactly what the user of ridicule wants.

Name calling often results from projection. People who see their own fears and failings in others may accuse the others of what the people themselves fear. Someone who is biased against certain races, for example, may accuse you of bias. You may find this disturbing, since most people have some conflicting feelings about members of other races. Therefore, ridiculers may be able to project onto you their own unfair feelings about others. But even if you do have some uncertainties of your own, that does not mean you would treat a member of another race unfairly. The projection-based name-calling trap is a potent one, because in recognizing a grain of truth in the projector's argument, you take the bait and become defensive—to the ridiculer's delight.

Reductio ad ridiculum, which is Latin for "reduction to the ridiculous" (also called *reductio ad absurdum* or "reduction to the absurd") is a favorite tactic of skilled wordsmiths who want to ridicule others. It involves taking a logical fallacy that follows the implications of your argument to an absurd consequence to make you appear ridiculous.

In nearly every aspect of society and across culture and time, ridicule works. Ridicule leverages the emotions and simplifies the complicated and takes on the powerful, in politics, business, law, entertainment, the media, literature, culture, sports and romance. Ridicule can tear down faster than the other side can rebuild. It can smash a theoretical or intellectual construct.

—J. Michael Waller
Fighting the War of Ideas Like Real War

In reduction to the ridiculous, the mocker shows that an absurd result follows from your stated opinion—with the objective of eliciting an emotional reaction in you and anyone listening. This may be achieved by extending your argument's logic in an extremely absurd way or by presenting the argument in an overly simplified way.

For example, someone arguing for higher taxes on the rich might say, "It's simple: raising tax rates always increases tax revenue." The *reductio ad absurdum* reply might be, "So if we raise tax rates to 100%, people will still work and companies will still operate even though the government takes all their money, right? Sure. Don't be absurd!"

An *ad hominem* argument, also known as *argumentum ad hominem* (Latin: "argument toward the person" or "argument against the person") is an argument that links the validity of a premise to an irrelevant characteristic or belief of the person advocating the premise—and not to the premise itself.

In an *ad hominem* attack, the person making the argument is attacked, rather than attacking the argument. Someone might say, "I imagine that someone like you would have no idea about how difficult this actually is." An ad hominem attack suggests that the person putting forward the argument is not qualified to make it, or not worthy of attention. It is generally considered an underhanded debating technique.

Challenging Credentials or Maturity

Another common form of ridicule is to challenge your credentials, maturity, or sanity. An opponent may say, "Geez, nobody believes in socialism after college. Grow up!" to your argument supporting an increase in the minimum wage. Your argument is ridiculed on the basis that having a view commonly associated with youth is somehow invalid. Trying to deride the authors, an opponent might say, "Hey, surely people like you with your PhDs must know . . . !" Here the argument is ridiculed by questioning credentials— while the argument itself is never directly addressed at all.

Satire

Satire is a broad term applied to literature that blends criticism, wit, and ironic humor with the aim of ridiculing or rebuking someone or something. The target of satire can be a person or thing. Jonathan Swift's savage essay *"A Modest Proposal"* targeted the Irish landowning system with the suggestion that the Irish handle famine by eating their own children. In our own time, the government and individual politicians are favorite targets of satire on television

shows such as *Saturday Night Live.*
Skilled wordsmiths often use satire
to ridicule divergent ideas and
actions. When called on it, they'll
defend themselves with "I was just
being satirical!" as if satirizing is
somehow more acceptable than
other forms of ridicule.

Satire blends criticism, wit, and ironic humor with the aim of ridiculing or rebuking someone or something.

It is useful to recognize the
various forms that ridicule can
take—but it is even more useful to know what to
do when you are subjected to ridicule. Ridicule
of any type is powerful because it either ignores
your thinking and questioning altogether or makes
your thoughts and questions seem so absurd that
they cannot and should not be taken seriously. To
question authority to think for yourself, you must
learn not only how to identify ridicule but also how to
handle it when you are subjected to it—as you almost
certainly will be if you advance divergent views.

20

Defeat Ridicule

Ridicule is so powerful because it simultaneously invokes so many different fears: fear of losing others' respect, of being considered contemptible and beneath notice, of being thought stupid, of being isolated and marginalized, of being ostracized. The fears alone can be so overwhelming that someone who has been ridiculed before for "contrary" opinions may be very reluctant ever to bring them up again. Ridicule is provocative as well as demeaning—but it is also very hard to ignore, which is why it is such an effective tactic for side-tracking and defeating you and your arguments. To foil the tactic of ridicule, it's helpful to remember how it works. Ridicule is a form of bullying, and bullies search out vulnerabilities, looking for your weaknesses. They goad you with taunts aimed at your sensitive spots until you crack and explode with anger—then the bully laughs as you freak out. The ridiculer has no interest in you as a person and none in your point of view—only in getting you to lose control so you appear hyper-emotional, unintelligent and unworthy of anyone's serious consideration.

Mockery is a rust that corrodes all it touches.
—Milan Kundera
Czech author

Ridicule is a kind of "bait" that your opponent puts out to ensnare you. If you take the bait and respond with anger or defensiveness, you lose, as your reaction is "goaded and guided" to make you look stupid and foolish. Mocking laughter is like waving the proverbial red flag in front of the bull, which then reactively paws the dirt and charges mindlessly with horns lowered. If you begin "seeing red," your opponent's ridicule has achieved its purpose. If you respond to the sneering and snickering, your opponent has succeeded in getting control of your reactions. The strength of ridicule lies not in what your opponent says but, always, in your reaction.

Especially in political debates, expert ridiculers attempt to draw their opponents into a defensive posture on the ridiculer's ground. It's a rhetorical trick, a sleight of hand. Defeating this sort of ridicule is not accomplished through defensive statements that attempt to argue the point raised by the ridiculer—defensive statements to refute the ridiculer's taunts simply reinforce the claims.

Side-Stepping the Ridicule Trap

Independent thinkers want, above all, to be taken seriously, to have their analyses and arguments considered as being well-reasoned and well-argued, even if the opponent or group ultimately does not accept them. Ridicule aims directly at this desire by trying to make it seem absurd that anyone would seriously consider paying attention to the independent thinker's "stupid" and "ridiculous" comments.

Fortunately for independent thinkers, there are a variety of ways to side-step the ridicule trap. The basic strategy is to ignore the bait. This is easy to say, but remaining detached and calm in the face of intense ridicule is no easy feat—it takes the mental control of a Zen Master. No matter how much you are goaded and bullied, laughed at and ridiculed, the best way to neutralize the sting of the ridicule is to ignore its temptation, refusing to respond to it.

The bait will be as provocative as opponents think they can get away with. Expect it. Opponents will use personal knowledge of anything especially hurtful to you for bait. Fishermen bait hooks with what gets the fish's attention—a worm, a fly, a lure; there are many possibilities. Your opponent does the same thing. Opponents use as bait whatever they think you can't ignore. While you may be very offended, keep in mind that the bait is not used to hurt you; its purpose is to hook you. Defending yourself is taking the bait.

Counter Tactic—Ignore the Ridicule

The most effective way to defeat ridicule is to ignore it. Do not respond. Remember ridicule is bait! You may give a knowing little laugh if you like, but remain calm. Ridicule is an attempt to cause you to replace reason with uncontrolled passion. Saul Alinsky, in *Rules for Radicals*, explained that the strength of ridicule lies not in the ridicule itself but in "the enemy's reaction." The purpose of ridicule is to provoke you into losing your cool so that you self-destruct. Do not take the bait. No matter how much you are goaded, bullied and laughed at, the answer to the temptation is to *refuse it.*

Counter Tactic—Surrender

Ridicule gets its power from your buying into it, so you accept the ridicule "as if it were true." The first urge is to argue, protest, and fight back, which is exactly what your opponent wants. Opponents seek emotional responses to get you going—to get you to put on your Red Hat. Once you respond emotionally, your opponent can guide your response to make you look and feel like a fool.

When you argue with ridicule, you've been sucked in and your opponent has prevailed. Instead, simply "accept" the ridicule as a statement among many statements. Surrender to the ridicule by not disagreeing with it, by not resisting it, by not responding to it. You can

The most effective way to defeat ridicule is to ignore it. Do not respond.

respond with such statements as, "You may be right," or "Maybe." If someone says, "You're so dumb. What a silly notion," you say, "Well, I may be dumb, but I still think that . . . ." The ridiculer retorts, "Yes, You are a total dummy." You can say, "Maybe it's a dumb idea, but I believe . . . ."

You surrender to ridicule in the sense that you do not respond; you do not take the bait. Instead, simply let it go. Let it pass by, without grabbing it. Voicing no disagreement or argument does not mean that you agree with the ridicule—although it may feel that way—but that's only because your ego took it as real.

Surrendering to being laughed at and having your opinions twisted and ridiculed is not a natural response, because we feel impelled to correct the wrong attribution. But doing what is natural is how we get ourselves hooked. The trick of being able to "accept" the ridicule is not to "buy into it." Buying in means to accept it as true of yourself, to believe it. Your "ego" trips you up. But you don't have to take everything people say about you as true. If someone said, "You're a Martian," which is absurd, must you refute it? You can simply ignore the comment without response. That does not mean that you agree that you're a Martian—does it?

Shrug Off the Ridicule

Shrug your shoulders. Look away. Don't look at a ridiculer. A ridiculer would love you to look at the sneer on his or her face. So, don't make eye contact. Act bored and make a dismissive statement such as, "I don't care," "So what," or "Doesn't matter."

> Ridiculer: Hey! You walk funny.
>> You (with a shrug): So what?
>> Ridiculer: Hey, dorky! Your shirt looks funny.
>> You (with a shrug): I don't care.

Poke Fun at Yourself

You can disarm ridiculers by agreeing with their taunts and going along with their gags. For example, when you are ridiculed, fake a cry and say something like, "Oh, you're really hurting my feelings." If a ridiculer calls you names, you may take a bow and say, "Thank you. Thank you very much. You are much too kind. I have been called worse."

> Ridiculer: You look like a penguin when you walk.
>> You: Thanks for noticing. I've been working hard on my penguin walk.
>> Ridiculer: Just look in the mirror -- you even look like a penguin.
>> You: Oh my gosh, you're right. Call my parents. Get me an airplane ticket to the South Pole, now.

Counter Tactic—Embrace It

Being laughed at and the "brunt of a joke" is intolerable, as Alinsky astutely observed. We respond with knee-jerk resistance and blowback. But with a little cleverness you can avoid going for the ridicule bait by doing the opposite of what your opponent expects—owning and embracing the ridicule.

The 2010 Senate race in Massachusetts, in which Republican Scott Brown snatched what had been

Ted Kennedy's seat, provided a wonderful example of side-stepping ridicule by embracing it. Brown had driven from campaign site to campaign site in his 2005 GMC pickup truck, which featured over 201,000 miles. Stumping for Brown's opposition, President Obama mocked Brown with, "Anybody can buy a truck!"

Instead of resisting and becoming annoyed, Brown embraced the ridicule and ran with it. "When he started to criticize my truck, that's where I drew the line," Brown joked, adding that when Obama called to offer congratulations after his victory, he offered to "drive the truck down to Washington so [the President] can see it." Brown's embrace of the ridicule was so powerful that for a while he began every speech with, "Hi, I'm Scott Brown and I drive a truck!" By owning the ridicule, Brown acquired a powerful metaphor for his unlikely journey to victory in the unlikeliest of states.

Another example is President Jimmy Carter, who was ridiculed as a rural peanut farmer by supposedly sophisticated urbanites. Carter embraced the ridicule, often being seen wearing a sweater rather than an urban-style suit and making frequent references to his hometown of Plains, Georgia. Peanuts became a frequent prop for Carter's campaigns and presidency, projecting a down-home, regular-guy atmosphere that, at least for a time, successfully connected with many Americans.

So when ridiculed, catch yourself going for the bait—catch yourself responding to the taunts with knee-jerk emotional resistance. Then step

All truths pass through three phases. First, it is ridiculed. Second, it is violently opposed. Third, it is accepted as self-evident.

—Arthur Schopenhauer

back and look for a way to embrace—to agree with—
the ridicule. Doing so will defuse the mockery and stop
your opponent.

Counter Tactic—Draw Out the Ridiculer

An alternative method for dealing with an opponent
who is emotional and angry is to draw the person out
with open questions, reflections, tentative summaries
("Do you mean . . .?") while resisting the temptation
to argue. This takes the wind out of opponents' sails.
They tend to calm down and talk normally. When
fully drawn out, the opponent will be more receptive
than initially. Drawing opponents out, rather than
arguing or presenting your view, provides you with all
kinds of information. Perhaps you have not actually
understood their position or have been misinformed
in the facts. You have several points to respond to
now or later.

Finally, drawing an opponent out communicates
openness as well as strength: the person feels
listened to and was listened to. You have provided no
resistance, yet you have not agreed to any of what
the opponent has said. Further, you hold the power.
You can respond now or you can put the opponent off
– "Hmmm, interesting. I'll get back to you on that."
Then you can leave—go dig up info, think over what
to do, do nothing. You have all the choices.

To be effective at drawing an opponent out, you
have to let go of the notion that you can "win the
argument." You won't. So if you aren't trying to win
the argument, then what is your goal? Try setting
yourself a goal of attempting to raise the other
person's awareness while maintaining your own
sense of inner peace. That is, focus on helping the
other person become more aware of the full extent
of their behavior and how it affects you and others,

but without taking ownership of anything the other person says. Never defend against any of their comments. Simply redirect the comments back to the person.

Some examples:

"How stupid are you?" "Well, I'm not sure. How stupid do you think I am?"

"That's the dumbest thing I've ever heard." "What makes it dumb?"

"That might work on Mars." "Do you mean it could work if things were different here?"

In other words, you don't attack—ever. Instead, deflect the other person's attacks back, over and over. Become like a mirror. So the more the other person tries to attack you, the more they weaken themselves. People can't punch themselves in the face for too long.

It is important not to give in and become sarcastic when deflecting comments back. It is very tempting to do so, but it undercuts your purpose, which is to evade the ridicule and make it ineffective. If you speak sarcastically, it will be obvious to the ridiculer and anyone else listening that something has "gotten to you" and made you upset or angry. Strive for the blandest possible delivery of your deflections—you can actually practice this by recording your voice, playing it back and listening to how you sound. If you speak with emotion or sarcasm, the ridiculer is winning by pulling you onto his turf and away from the points you are trying to make. Remember the "you're a Martian" example—a statement so ridiculous that there is no need to refute it. Consider the ridiculer's statements as if they are just as ridiculous as saying "you're a Martian." Then you will not feel you need to argue back, deny or make a sarcastic response; you can simply let the statements pass through you as a knife passes through water without harming the water in any way.

Other Counter Tactics

Take an argument about global warming as an example. A cow's burps and gas emissions add 70 to 120 kilograms of methane—a greenhouse gas—to the atmosphere every year. The effects of methane are 23 times stronger than the effects of carbon dioxide, which is often blamed for global warming. So 100 kg of methane has the same effect as 2300 kg of carbon dioxide, which is approximately the amount generated by driving a car 7,800 miles per year. Leave out how much this matters—just imagine a ridiculer using the information against you during a debate:

> "Great! Cow farts cause global warming! So you're saying we should ban cows!"

Agree ... but

Here you agree with the person's comment quickly and then repeat your point. "Yes, cows and agriculture do contribute to global warming, but they are only one small part of a big picture. The major factor contributing to warming is ....."

Ask for Clarification

Another way to defuse ridicule is to respond to it as if the comment is serious and ask that the ridiculer clarify what they mean in saying it. Suppose you are discussing why global warming is a problem and someone snickers, "Well, we'll have to ban cows with all of that farting and methane gas output!" You might respond with, "Ban cows? How would that work?"

Stick to the Facts, Ma'am

Put on your White Hat. Ignore the ridicule and state
the facts and statistics. The purpose of ridicule is
to get your ire up. You defeat the ridiculer when you
respond by coolly saying facts. It leaves the ridiculer
looking foolish.

Expect Attacks

If you question authority to think for yourself,
expect to be ridiculed—and immunize yourself. You
will be vilified, so prepare. What is the worst thing
that an adversary can say? You will be tested. After
all, you are questioning authority, which makes
people, especially those in authority, profoundly
uncomfortable. Do not be surprised if they seek
to make you uncomfortable in return—and do not
be surprised if they don't "fight fair." After all,
authorities want to protect their position and their
viewpoint, and the faster and more effectively they
can marginalize anyone who questions them, the less
likely it will be that other people will ask unwanted
questions.

21

Question Authors

It is no accident that the words "author" and "authority" are so similar. Both derive from the same Latin root: *auctor,* meaning founder, master or leader—literally "one who causes to grow," from the word *auctus,* a form of the verb "to increase." The idea that an authority has "the power to enforce obedience" is much later, dating to the 14th century.

As authors of this book, our purpose is to encourage you to grow—to question authority to think for yourself, to analyze things in your own way, decide what is important to you, accept "common wisdom" only when your own thinking and analysis lead you to believe that what "everyone knows" is in fact what makes sense to you.

We have urged you to question authority, to understand some of the means by which authorities seek to suppress questioning, manipulate people into making predetermined decisions, and exact behavior that is sheeplike (turning people into "sheeple") rather than the behavior of fully human and self-directing beings. Authority is not always wrong and does not always have nefarious motivations, but it is *sometimes* wrong and *sometimes* ill-motivated. Even when well-motivated, its dictates may not be right for you. How will you know when authority is benevolent and when it is not if you do not question it at every opportunity?

Begin your journey into becoming a skilled independent thinker by questioning us, your authors, who have set ourselves up as authorities on questioning authority to think for yourself. We tell you that our motivations are positive and benign, but why believe us? Our motivations may be noble, but still, what we suggest must work for you. Question our authority and the material in this book. Don't just accept ideas and recommendations suggested in this book. Use the techniques recommended to decide for yourself if they work for you. Add your own experiences and insights to information from this book and added material you dig up on your own, to test the ideas and to develop your own methods of questioning authority to think for yourself. While practicing the techniques in this book, you'll likely evolve methods that work better for you. Questioning authority to think for yourself is crucial to living the life of a full, free human being, no matter what methods of questioning work best for you. Go find them!

There is nothing wrong with holding an opinion and holding it passionately. But at those times when you're absolutely sure that you're right, talk with someone who disagrees. And if you constantly find yourself in the company of those who say "Amen" to everything that you say, find other company.

—Condoleezza Rice

The world is a dangerous place to live, not because of the people who are evil, but because of the people who don't do anything about it.

—Albert Einstein

Our lives begin to end the day we remain silent about things that matter.

—Martin Luther King Jr.

Authors

Beverly A. Potter, Ph.D, (Docpotter) received her doctorate in counseling psychology from Stanford University and her masters in vocational rehabilitation counseling from San Francisco State University. She is a self-help author noted for challenging rules and thinking of issues from a fresh perspective. Her work  blends philosophies of humanistic psychology, social learning theory and Eastern philosophies to create an inspiring and original approach to handling the many difficulties encountered today. Beverly provides keynote speeches and training. Her offices are in Oakland, California. (www.docpotter.com)

Mark James Estren, Ph.D, received his doctorates in psychology and in English from University of Buffalo and his master's degree in journalism from Columbia University. He is a Pulitizer-Prize-winning journalist who has held top-level positions at several newspapers and TV news organizations for over 30 years, including *The Washington Post, Miami Herald, Philadelphia Inquirer, CBS* and *ABC News* and other news media. He was one of *Fortune* magazine's "People to Watch". Early in his career Mark ran *Financial News Network* and was the editor of *High Technology Business* magazine. Mark's offices are in Ft. Myers, Florida. (www.markjestren.com)

RONIN BOOKS FOR INDEPENDENT MINDS

HIGH PERFORMANCE GOAL SETTING ....Potter HIGOAL 9.95 ___
How to use intuition to conceive and achieve your dreams.
GET PEAK PERFORMANCE EVERY DAY ....Potter GETPEA 12.95 ___
How to manage like a coach.
FINDING A PATH WITH A HEART ....Potter FINPAT 14..95 ___
How to go from burnout to bliss, principles of self-leading.
THE WAY OF THE RONIN ....Potter WAYRON 14.95 ___
Maverick career strategies for riding the waves of change.
FROM CONFLICT TO COOPERATION ....Potter FROCON 14.95 ___
How to mediate a dispute, step-by-step technique.
MANAGING YOURSELF FOR EXCELLENCE ....Potter MANYOU 12.95 ___
How to become a Can-Do person.
WORRYWART'S COMPANION ....Potter WORWAR 12.95 ___
21 ways to soothe yourself and worry smart.
OVERCOMING JOB BURNOUT ....Potter OVEJOB 14.95 ___
How to renew enthusiasm for working. Principles of self-management
FUGITIVE PHILOSOPHER. ....Leary FUGPHI 12.95___
Story of Tim Leary's amazing life.
START YOUR OWN RELIGION................................... Leary STAREL 14.00 ___
Do it yourself religion.
TURN ON TUNE IN DROP OUT .... Leary TURNON 12.95 ___
Leary's classic manual on dropping out.

Books prices: SUBTOTAL $_____

CA customers add sales tax 8.75% _____
BASIC SHIPPING: (All orders) $.600

PLUS SHIPPING: { USA+$1 for each book, Canada+$2 for each book, Europe+$7 for each book, Pacific+$10 for each book }
Books + Tax + Basic + Shipping: TOTAL $_____

Checks/Money Order Payable to Ronin Publishing

MC _ Visa _ Exp date __ - __ card #: _ _ _ _ _ _ _ _ _ _ _ _ _ _ _ _ _ _ (sign) _ _ _ _ _ _ _ _ _ _ _ _ _

Name_ _

Address _ City _ _ _ _ _ _ _ _ _ _ _ _ _ _ _ _ State _ _ _ ZIP_____

Call for our FREE catalog. On-line catalog-> www.roninpub.com

& Orders (800)858-2665 • Info (510)420-3669 • Fax (510)420-3672
Available at amazon.com or order through your independent bookstore.
Ask your library to add Docpotter's books to their collection.